Twilight Sparkle: I left her in good hands.
Rainbow Dash: What are "hands"?
—*My little Pony: Equestria Girls*

"Get your stinking paws off me you damn dirty apes!"
— *Planet of the Apes*

"Maybe all along I was meant to be a fish."
— *The Incredible Mr. Limpet*

"You're even beginning to look like a rabbit!"
—*Bugs Bunny*

Cthulhu: I have seen the picture of what you claim is my spawn. That is not
my son. You madam, put a diaper on an octopus to perpetrate your fraud in
the first picture and in the second have stapled a squid to a doll's face.
— *Patrick Thomas' **Dear Cthulhu***

"The human world, it's a mess…"
—Disney's *The Little Mermaid*

"Grandmother, what big teeth you have!"
—*Little Red Riding Hood*

I… am… Batman!
—*Batman Beyond*

I love being a turtle!
—*Teenage Mutant Ninja Turtles*

Wesley: Charles, you just peed on my shoes.
—*Angel*

Danny: How does the kitty-cat go?
Max: M-m-meow?
—*Cats Don't Dance*

Lily: What'd they do? Rub your belly? Give you a dragon treat?
—*Once Upon a Time*

It's not easy being green.
—*Kermit the Frog*

You must summon your inner unicorn.
—*Phoebe and Her unicorn*

She's married to Roger Rabbit!?
—*Who Framed Roger Rabbit*

I think we're looking for some kind of genetic freak…
— *The X-Files*

They [humans] only exist in stories.
—*Ferngully The Last Rainforest*

There wolf. There castle.
—*Young Frankenstein*

Goliath: I never realized, when you were human, how beautiful you are.
Elisa: You mean you thought I was ugly?
—*Gargoyles*

Beast: I wasn't always so hairsuit.
—*X-men (The Animated Series)*

No-no. Not animal possession, ***animal possession***. Demonic possession. The possession of the spirit by an animal.
—*Wolf*

I will not turn into a snake. It never helps.
—*Peter Anspach (The Evil Overlord List)*

Other Books By This Author

How to Be an Anime Character

Lesbian Fairy Tales

Undead Strippers Versus the Alien Zombie Queen

Yes Virginia, There Is A Bogeyman

Yokai Manor

The Fool's Handbook

Harlequin: A Fool's World Novel

Furries

A Guide to Anthropomorphism
By, Clayton Overstreet

Contents

A Brief Introduction to Anthropomorphism

Anthropomorphism: The practice of ascribing human
characteristics to non-human things.

It's a broad topic and encompasses literally *everything*. Humans
have ascribed their own characteristics to all things in the universe
from atoms to galaxies. According to many religions everything in
the world has its own spirit. People looking up at the sky have seen
human shapes in everything from the stars to the clouds. The same
for mountains, rocks, trees, and food. Like in *Alice in Wonderland*
where everything from cards to door knobs came to life. Religious
figures are often seen appearing on tortillas for example. Ancient
legends speak of a man who carved a statue of his ideal woman
which was brought to life by the gods to love him or the golem
who was brought to life to do men's bidding. In modern times you
can see cartoons in which just about anything can talk and find
crazy men living on the street who have animated discussions with
mail boxes or thin air. You have probably tried talking to your own
pets or toys or maybe a motion picture screen, despite knowing
that they can never understand or answer you.
Discussing every aspect of this in detail would take a lifetime. So
instead this book focuses on animal anthropomorphism, or as it is
known today "Furries", which refers to both the phenomenon itself
and those who support it. The practice of combining human and
animal traits. Alternatively loved and reviled, especially on the
Internet, up until now the only books on the subject have been on
drawing them or chapters in psychological text books. In this book

we'll discuss what furries are, what they aren't, where they came from, and their various aspects. How they appear in the lives of nearly everyone, whether they recognize it or not, and always have. If you have tried explaining it to other you can show them this book. If you want to understand it yourself, read on.
But beware. Once you begin down this road you may never be able to turn back.

What Are Furries?

There is some debate as to what actually qualifies as a "furry". Mostly by people who do not want to admit that they are furries. Anime fans love catgirls, various combinations of felines and various other animals with women, yet will argue against furries claiming that they are excepted because they just have the cat/dog/whatever ears, tail, claws, fangs, and eyes but say not a coat of fur. Of course they also argue the difference between anime and cartoons which makes about as much sense. Some claim that werewolves and other shape shifters do not count because they spend time completely human on the outside, regardless of whatever other form they may take. That centaurs do not count because part of them is completely human while from the waist down they are completely animal. Or a hundred other exceptions. This book will not get bogged down in semantics. I'll present all of the options and let you decide what "counts". Though it is not just creatures with fur, but also birds, reptiles, dinosaurs, fish, mollusks, one celled organisms, insects, plants, artificial intelligences, and any other living thing.

Standard Furries

The basic furry form is a human shape with a more animal like head. Their skin is either furry, scaly, or feathered even if it's only a thin coating. Sometimes it just stops there. Mostly it continues on with other changes. The heads are normally shaped like snouts or beaks, but with the ability to show all the same emotions as a human. Their eyes, teeth, tongues, and noses can be either human or animal. The ears are usually more animal-like. Hair is optional on the head, though most times only females have long hair rather than thicker fur or lengthened scales and feathers.

Only the more animal-shaped furries have paws or hooves for hands (though this rarely seems to stop them from making clothes, using tools, cooking food, and all those other human things). Those shaped more human have fingers numbering from three thick ones to the more normal four (which are easier to draw) or the human five, usually with an opposable thumb in there somewhere and animal-like pads for finger tips. About 90% of the ones with fingers also have pointy claws instead of finger nails, depending on species.

Tails are almost a requirement in any furry, whether they have human legs or not if the species has one. Gorillas for example do not get one, but a fish-girl would have one sticking out behind her… though that can be replaced by webbed feet or fins that they can somehow walk on if they are on land. If they are completely aquatic they might not even have feet. A snake woman might have a tail between her legs or just be a snake from the waist down. Arms are also optional based on species, but may be a combination of arms and wings or arms and more snakes or tentacles.

How exactly the animals combine with the human form varies from creature to creature.

Ordinary Animals

Sometimes their owners dress them up in costumes and clothes and they do tricks, but they don't really count as furries. Some of them like gorillas, dolphins, some pigs, and a few birds can be intelligent, but this is their own ability and is not a combination of human and animal traits.

Humans

A lot of furries are humans in costumes, who are highly interested in furries, want a physical or emotional relationship with a furry, or who wear clothes with images of furries on them. Or just animal ears on a headband. Superheroes and Villains often wear costumes based on animals too and can fall into this category. If they have powers that go with the costume that's just gravy, though just as many dress up as animals to scare superstitious and cowardly criminals or ordinary citizens.

(See other chapters for more details on this).

Then you have humans who think like animals. Raised by wolves or other animals like the founder of Rome Romulus or Pecos Bill or Mowgli, living so long away from humans that they have lost the normal socializing skills and act like animals, experimented on or tortured or diseased until they are driven mad until they become beasts themselves.

The same thing happens to animals raised by humans.

Intelligent Animals

These are basically animals who are as smart as humans and may have some of their facial expressions. Like ducks who can smile, dogs who can snicker, or horses who can do a raspberry. (Thhppppp!) They demonstrate an obvious knowledge of what is going on and an intent in their actions, often even seeming to understand what people say or intentionally ignoring them. Like when Sea Monkeys and Germs under microscopes spell out "moron" when you look at them, a dog is caught with a pencil in his mouth writing, or a canary opens its cage and flies off to lead the gas inspector back to the mine. They may even have their own universal language that is understood by all animals except humans.

A lot of mythical creatures fall into this category like dragons, unicorns, foxes, and the like. The same for horror movie animals that hunt down specific people and murder them rather than just the standard instincts of a dumb animal.

Talking Animals

One step up from Intelligent Animals people have imagined being
able to communicate with animals since the dawn of time. Usually
so we can get them to do things for us, train them easier, berate
them for doing things we do not like, or so we can have friends
who aren't as lame as human beings. In ancient times it was
believed that drinking the blood of a dragon allowed you to talk to
birds. Fairy tales are full of helpful animals that lead people out of
trouble or who were once humans who were transformed. And
many modern day children's stories are told with entire casts of
animals, either one species or several,
living in communities together.

Unintelligent Furries

Some furries have human traits or are fully human in form, but remain mentally animals. This is different from Ordinary Animals because while not intelligent they have hands or maybe fully human bodies with animal brains stuck in them by aliens or mad scientists. A few of them actually share brain space with a human mind. Maybe in a split personality like a werewolf.

Man Beasts

Creatures with a definite split between their human and animal
forms. Like a centaur or a mermaid which is human from the waist
up and animal below. Harpies and Sphinxes which have the heads
and sometimes the breasts of women but are fully animals
otherwise. Some born from the blood of the gods themselves, the
result of curses like when a man who made a play for the queen of
the fairies was given a donkey's head and Medusa whose hair was
made of snakes, or breeding among monsters
like Echidna and Typhon.

Fairies

Either because they are spirit beasts, elementals, or from alternate worlds fairies have always had combinations of human and animal traits. Pixies have insect wings like dragonflies or butterflies. Elves have cat-like eyes and pointed ears and in older stories may have had fur, cow tails, and some even had hooves, wings, or horns.

Shape Shifters

Ideally able to take any form they want when they want, be it human, animal, or any combination of them without any problems and maintaining their ability to think like a human with possibly gaining animal instincts. Others change or are transformed against their will, sometimes in excruciating pain as their insides and bones are rearranged into new shapes, and possibly losing all semblance of humanity like a rampaging werewolf.
Or any combination there of.

Gods, Demons, & Spirits

Various entities are either born or take on forms in our world or the
spirit world that appear to be animal forms or combinations of
humans and animals. Angels for example are described most often
as humans with wings, but can also have multiple heads of
different animals and various other shapes. Demons are often
pictured with hooves, bat wings, and horns. Gods sometimes have
antlers or look completely human. Some spirits have no form until
they take on the shape of something else or may not actually look
like animals, but appear that way to humans whose minds interpret
them in a way we can understand. But since they are born that way
and in many cases predate the existence of mortal animals you
can't really say they look like said animals,
but that the animals look like them.
Sometimes gods lose or never learned the ability to change shapes.
Pan for example always appeared as a satyr.

Chimeras

Originally the Chimera was a rabid fire breathing indestructible monster with the head and body of a lion, a second head of a goat, and a tail that was a living viper. Now the word is used for creatures that combine the DNA and traits of several different species. Like if an animal had a snake's body, a cat's head, and a goat's horns.

Robots and Cyborgs

There are a variety of robots that can take on both animal and
human form. There may be a group of them that are normally
animal shaped, but can combine into giant sword wielding
warriors, usually piloted by humans with powers similar to the
animals the robots resemble. Animals and humans can be
augmented, given cybernetic parts that can make them resemble
other animals or think in other ways from nanites
to prosthetic limbs or organs.

Tentacle Beasts

Creatures that either have tentacles or are mostly if not entirely
made up of them. They can also be more liquid in form and able to
form tentacles but do not normally have them
or just sprout them when needed.

Plants

Some furries are plants, not animals. Dryads are a prime example.
Thumbelina from Hans Christian Anderson's story of the same
name and a princess in Japan were born of them and then there are
talking or even walking trees, humanoid plants,
flowers with faces, and so on.

Original Creatures

Extremely rare sometimes people come up with completely new and unique animals that do not resemble anything in nature. I can't describe them, but you'll know them when you see them. Sometimes they are furries by themselves and other times they get combined with humans like the rest

.

Parallel Evolution

It is theorized that aliens on other planets might resemble humans
or animals. Many superheroes in comics represent this when they
arrive on Earth. Stories of alien abduction often feature gray aliens
with big black eyes that are still amazingly human shaped. And
almost all stories involving aliens or monsters have some sort of
alien-human or monster-human hybrid running around the place
who is the result of a Romeo and Juliet style romance or some
experiment/dark magic. Which would mean they would be furries
even if they *look* completely human.
Technically aliens would not resemble creatures on Earth any more
than we would resemble them. Why this would happen would be
because similar things, like hands, are required for similar actions
like gripping things. Also there are some theories and even
religions that say life may have originated on other worlds.

Elementals

Some of these creatures have a non-organic component too them, especially in Japanese children's shows. A furry might be shaped like animals/humans, but are made out of earth, fire, water, wind, or other inorganic components. However if they do not have both human-like traits and animal traits they do not count as furries.

Animal Symbolism

Since the beginning of humanity we have always imitated animals. Some of the oldest cave paintings ever found depict a man in animal skins dancing about. Feathers have been used by tribes across the world for head dresses and masks or face paint used to endow shamans and warriors with aspects of the animals they resemble. The oldest of gods always seem to resemble animals and to this day people do their best to draw aspects of animals into their lives. From rooftop gargoyles to the shields and helmets of knights. Traditionally for protection and to instill confidence. Here are a few modern examples of how human and animals are combined every day.

Martial Arts

Starting centuries ago rulers came up with the idea of removing weapons from the hands of peasants to make them easier to control. Said peasants realized that outlaws and abusive nobles, who do not really obey laws banning weapons, would have an unfair advantage over law abiding citizens. So they observed animals and copied their motions to develop fighting styles like Kung Fu still used today in your local dojo.

Clothes and Accessories

While Furries tend to dress up as their favorite animals, often home made, there isn't a costume shop in the world that would be without one or two animal outfits. Werewolves, cat girls, frog princes, television characters, elves and reindeer for Christmas, the Easter Bunny, and more. A lot of stores even sell hats, hoodies, and accessories with animal ears, eyes, or fangs.

A lot of clothes have cartoon animals emblazoned on them and nearly everyone has some jewelry in the shape of animals, animal heads, paw prints, eyes, or more. And a car isn't a car without its hood ornament.

Mascots

Be it the symbol and mascot of a sports team, a company logo,
toys, the box of cereal in your cupboard, or the coins in your
pocket there are a thousand things you see every day that have
animal if not actual furry symbols. Though there is always a furry
version of just about all of them somewhere.

Astrology and Astronomy

Humans have anthropomorphized even the stars in the sky. Huge balls of plasma so big and powerful that they can be seen from billions of miles away billions of years after their light had ceased to shine. When they die they explode so powerfully that they vaporize anything else for millions of miles and then collapse in on themselves and tear holes through the very fabric of reality that pull in anything that gets close and compresses it in a gravity well that not even light can escape.

Before we knew that though, we only knew that celestial bodies floated as tiny points of light above us forming patterns in the night sky. Placed there by the gods each had its story. A nymph seduced by a goddess and wrongly accused of infidelity and turned into a bear. A dragon that stretched across the sky. A centaur armed with arrows and wisdom. A faithful hound who refused to leave his master. A man in the moon… or is it a rabbit?

Then there came the astrological signs that supposedly rule human lives. Rams, fish, goats, crabs, tigers, birds… each one assigned to a person at the moment of their birth in every culture around the world. To this day people read their horoscopes every day in newspapers and magazines or even pay money for mystics and scientists to give them a more personal prediction.

What's your sign?

Food

Animal shaped crackers/cookies, pancakes with mouse ears, candy, cereal, raisins on celery, and just about everything else a person could eat has animal connotations whether it is made from animals or not. Not to mention how you eat it be it like a pig, bear, horse, bird, or more. You are what you eat after all.

There are two basic ways to interpret the rest of the furry symbolism and each gets its own section because they are diametrically opposed. Mysticism and Religion state that there are powers far beyond the every day which are deeply connected to animals, humans, and the deeper meaning behind all things in the universe and that we can tap into this by performing rites, wearing masks, and doing our best to understand the numinous. Psychology claims that this is all in our heads and that people have all kinds of mental needs and problems and that the how and why of furries are ways of dealing with that.
So we will discuss each one on its own and let you decide which one is the right one or a combination of the two.

Furry Mysticism & Religion

While humans like to think of themselves as having the ability to understand reality and how it works, we are at best dealing with severely limited information based solely on observed evidence. Up until a relatively short time ago we thought diseases were caused by evil fairies and have alternatively declared the sun to be a giant gold ball pulled by a god in a chariot, a flaming bird, a god in its own right, the center of the solar system, a star, fire, gas, and plasma just to name a few. Even today many people seek information about the world around us in alternative ways to the scientific method. Preferably by contacting beings who know more than us and can simply tell us what we want to know or need to do Focusing on what this has to do with furries leads to the following topics. Any of which could drive a person to try to recreate these things.

Gods, Devils, & Spirits

One can barely think of the idea of human-animal forms without thinking of the gods. Particularly those of ancient Egypt. While most religions started off worshipping gods in the form of various animals (possibly in the hopes that our tiny naked cave dwelling ancestors who had no claws or fangs could convince them not to devour us in the night) the Egyptians took it and their empire to new heights that are remembered to this day even though some other religions have tried to destroy anything that says the creator of the universe resembles any creature but humans or that the universe exists for anyone but us.

Not so different from the gods Devils are beings who have many of the same qualities, but who are largely considered opposed to the happiness of humanity, ranging from mischief and pranks to the destruction of all existence.

Between them are other spirits. Ghosts and the souls of the dead who have various possible afterlives, but who sometimes contact the living or are contacted by them. The same for animal spirits or smaller gods who are not quite as powerful as the earth shaking Titans. Witches often call such spirits to appear or take the form of animals as their familiars and some families have guardian spirits who have for various reasons agreed to protect them.

One of the best ways to contact these beings is through the law of similarity, a mystical belief hat the image of something can create a link to the real thing. Masks, totems, statues, and amulets. Entire temples are built and blessed around such images as are cemeteries. Others find them to be natural places deep in the woods away from humanity where they can find such spirits connected to the natural environment. People will then meditate, chant the name of a spirit that they might know, and partake in various "herbs" to try to evoke and connect with them to beg favors or make deals.

Tulpas

Some speculate that some if not all mystical beings only exist
because we believe they do. Even some sciences like quantum
physics claim that all we see and experience is a shared dream,
meant to allow us to live in a world which would otherwise make
no sense. We cannot even be sure the person next to us sees the
world the same way do… or that they exist at all. So by focusing
our energies it may be possible to change
or even create that dream.
A tulpa is a thought form. An imaginary friend who through the
power of belief becomes more real. Safer to deal with than other
gods in some ways because it is what you make it, but beware.
Like Frankenstein's monster and so many others such beings start
out as what you imagine, but the longer they exist and the more
people believe in them the more self contained they become. Soon
they can come to chafe at their creator's commands, particularly
when they are envisioned to be gods. Whether they come to life
separate from their makers or simply find other people to believe
in them, it may not be long before they seek to destroy any who
know their true origins and instead rely on those who merely wish
to serve rather than control.
It is believed that enough people's belief can
bring to life nearly anything.

Possession & Invocation

Whatever their origins spirits do not always make their own bodies but take those of others. Ghosts, gods, demons, and even animal spirits all have been known to hijack the body of a human being for their own uses. There are hundreds of missionaries every year who come back with takes of such things. Shamans and priests are contacted to drive the spirits out, for depending on its strength the human they possess begins to act a lot less human. Some have been known to be driven to devour their fellow man or harm themselves as they are pushed to do things the human body was never meant for.

In more controlled situations though, a man might seek to allow such a spirit access. With proper rituals and spells one can invoke the spirits and even control them. This however is a balancing act as the spirits may resent this control or worse the person doing it cannot handle them.

Not all human spirits remain human. From various mystical energies to their own desires, they can change into other forms. Why not? They no longer have a body holding them in one shape. Whether this change is for good or bad depends.

Spells & Curses

Manipulating power can always have effects, whether intended or not. Some believe that merely contacting various mystical energies can affect a person. Mutating their body like radiation, warping their mind as they contact and learn of things man was never meant to know, or drawing the attention of beings who find toying with mortals very entertaining. A man could be cursed into a form other than human, his soul warped, his mind destroyed.

On the other hand some people seek such effects. Either to inflict them on others or experience it for themselves. In hundreds of cultures, many which never had anything to do with the others, it is believed that animal skins and the proper spells can allow a person to transform from human to animal form. Only a short time ago in Africa men were arrested after police witnessed them turning into crocodiles. On dark nights in the American Southwest people claim that skinwalkers will attack travelers, sometimes turning into huge wolves and running alongside vehicles speeding down the highway, gas pedals pressed to the floor without losing them. Throughout history there are also tales that such powers can have effects that extend beyond death, trapping souls in the Earthly planes or less savory parts of creation.

Monsters

There are dozens of ways for monsters to enter the world. The children of spirits or other monsters may be monsters. For every demigod born of the union of the gods and mortal or other beings, there is a monster. Loki for example has given rise to giant wolves, huge serpents, and a horse with a lot of extra legs. When one god kills another their blood tends to spawn all kinds of things. Or when they get mad they tend to turn the people who piss them off into anything they can come up with.

The original monsters though were created by Tiamat, the goddess of primal chaos (not to be confused with anarchy) mother of all gods when they killed her husband and turned on her, fearful that she would destroy them. When many of her children turned against her she created all kinds of monsters to help fight them. Scorpion men, bull men like the minotaur, dragons, demons, rabies, and more. She was eventually destroyed, but some of the monsters survived the war. Some even agreed to work for the gods while others fight on or went on to do their own thing.

Then you have the undead. Restless souls of expired humans who rise from their graves. Often in the search for blood, human flesh, the life force of living humans. Other souls, or revenge. Some are cursed into their undead form for some transgression or exposure to too much magic while alive. Ghouls are reputed to take the form of jackals or black dogs. Vampires can take on seemingly limitless other forms. Some without their own bodies will hijack and change others. Eating human flesh tends to make this outcome much more likely. Though at the same time Jesus told us to eat his in order to live forever in paradise.

Reincarnation

The mystical version of déjà vu there is a widespread belief that after a person dies they can come back in another body. The ultimate goal of this process is to become a god and thus earn a place in paradise. However the ways to do this are two ways to do this. One, be such a good and saintly person that you attain enlightenment and either rise to the level of the gods or your soul becomes one with the entirety of existence. Or two, do something that so impresses the gods that they want to keep you around.
Failing that and after a brief stay in some form of Hell (usually quite a bit more boring than the Christian version unless you did something really bad or piss off a god) to earn off a bit of your karmic debt for anything bad you may have done in life you come back either as a human or an animal. What animal may depend on what you want or what you do not want, depending on how good or bad you were in life. Relatively good people might get to be an eagle, a cow, a lion, or something impressive. Relatively bad people would probably be lucky to become a slug, a germ, or an ant, and hopefully get a better deal the next time.
Of course many furries would love to become an animal, but there are problems with the process. First of all, there is little if any proof that it actually works that way and any attempts to kill yourself usually counts against your soul. Second, you have to die. Combined with problem one, most people are content to wait to find out how the afterlife really works. Third, to become an animal one has to give up all the benefits of being human. Television, shopping, cooked food, and not running around on a leash as a consequence of living indoors. Sure spending your days as a cat lounging in the sun while a human opens a can of tuna for you sounds but, but not life in an alleyway eating trash. Also having your IQ go down from 100 to 34 seems a little "Flowers for

Algernon" to many and is not something most people are rushing
to embrace no matter how much they like animals.
Or it works the other way. A person could have memories of the
animal they were before hey moved "up" the ladder. Strange
feelings or vague memories that they may have been a cat, a shark,
or something else. The urge to return to their previous lifetime's
habits and desires as they find that humanity
leaves something to be desired.

Furry Psychology:
Humans VS Animals

Since we have little if any proof of the mystic forces of the world and are a cynical race, humans next turn to psychology. The study of the secrets hidden in that wet lump of gray matter behind the eyes which peers at the world through a limited view through five limited senses while at the same time looking inward for the meaning of it all and mostly keeping the parts of us that are more dangerous to ourselves and others in check as best it can. We think of these as our animal sides, but truthfully humans are capable of horrors that no animal would even contemplate. Goodness too, but that seems much rarer on most days.

Is it any wonder that some seek to connect more with other creatures in the hopes of finding something better? Physically we are soft creatures, easily hurt and without weapons nearly incapable of defending ourselves. Up until a few thousand years ago we were naked apes who were having trouble deciding between living in trees or on the ground. Our days consisted of finding food or avoiding being food. Even today most of the creatures in our grocery stores are the ones that cannot run or fly very well.

Then we invented fire, sharp rocks, and the wheel. After that natural selection took its course. We went from second to the bottom to the top of the food chain practically over night. In the years since we've gone from fearing the great predators to deciding which ones belong on the endangered species list and need us to

keep them from going extinct. Legally most animals are not even
allowed to live if they taste human flesh.
Yet now that we sit here as the dominant species of the planet we
have time to regret our place. To look around at what we have
made of the world and wonder if someone else could have done
better. Being human even with all our benefits largely sucks.
Sadly, like democracy, there are not a lot of other options
and few if any better ones.
Which does not prevent people from trying to come up with them.
The following are some of the mental reasons
people turn to being furries.

Man's Inhumanity To Man

There has always been a search for other intelligent life and the hope that if it exists it is better than us. The Native Americans have many wonderful stories of how nice it is to meet new friends from far away places. Those that survived anyway.

It has often been pointed out that while animals do have their conflicts, man, ants, and a handful or others are the only ones that engage in war. Man has taken it a few steps further and invented rape, torture, biological warfare, genocide, and more fun things. Our reasons for committing these crimes are unproven faiths, skin color, hair color, sexual orientation, demented joy in inflicting sadistic destruction and harm to others, psychological problems, tradition, convoluted plans, games, conflict of interest, and profit. Humans are basically born homicidal and it is a good thing that we have years of being trained out of that by adults. It's just too bad it is a process of trial and error. Strangely despite having been killing each other pretty much since we first came up with the club this seems to do nothing to curb our reproducing ourselves until there are currently about seven billion of us on the planet and growing. Sadly peaceful groups of humans have proven remarkably easy for everyone else to wipe from the face of the planet.

Then we look at the natural world that, until we got our hands on fire, had developed a nearly perfect equilibrium. Sure there were extinctions before and all kinds of changes, but before humans set foot on America there were enough trees that if it wanted a squirrel could go from one coat to the other without touching ground.

Nearly all of which have been cut down and paved over.

Animals do not need clothes. They can eat raw meat. They have claws and fangs so they do not need weapons. Many suspect that if

they were as smart as us they could do things differently. Better.
Without harming the world or each other the way we do.
Or that if we had their natural advantages to augment our own or
that they had our brains then they or we might do the same things
only a bit more viciously. If a cow could eat you, would it?

Lycanthropy and Rabies

Not everyone who acts like an animal has a choice. There is a psychological condition named Lycanthropy after the Greek king Lycos who was turned into a wolf. A person begins to act like an animal. Or at least how they think an animal would act. Some believe this is the origin of many tales of werewolves and possession. Usually they can become quite a bit more vicious than the actual animal.

Then there are physical diseases rather than mental ones that have a similar effect. Primarily among these is rabies. It slowly affects the mind until the person who contracts it is little more than an animal and through some mechanism drives them to bite others in order to propagate.

Suspension of Disbelief

In order to make someone learn or believe something new you have to get them to give up the feeling that the thing is impossible in the first place. To do that you start by getting someone to believe something smaller and a tried and true way for storytellers to do that has always been with talking animals. Aesop did it thousands of years ago, instilling morals into people through his animal tales. As have Hans Christian Anderson, the Brothers Grimm, and the creators of modern day cartoons. For if people can be convinced that an animal can talk or that a person can become one, what else in contrast seems impossible?
What else might be possible?
To escape from a reality someone finds displeasing even if only in their own heads some would try anything. Starting with a talking or even humanoid animal can be a good first step to at least developing a daydream in which you are happier.

Power & Fear

Humans are weak creatures. Some are weaker than others and from the beginning of time we have wondered what we could do with the abilities other animals display. Oh certainly there are some who have natural strength and skills or who develop them, but for the most part by comparison there are always things they have that we lack. Imagine if you could pick and choose from among them the things you wanted. Fur to keep you warm. Claws or venom to use in a fight. Faster reflexes. Greater strength or senses. The ability to fly on your own or disappear like a chameleon. Become impossible to catch or hurt. Live forever. Get revenge on those who treated you wrong. Or just have a few cosmetic changes that make you seem more attractive or at least unusual, so that you no longer blend in with the crowd. Maybe to make everyone that way, so that you finally can be different and still fit in.
The possibilities seem limitless and anyone who has been on the wrong end of a snarling dog knows the kind of power they have. On the other claw, people like to be scared. So many monsters collects the worst aspects of humans and animals. It is one thing when you are being chased by a vicious beast that wants to rend you limb from limb. It is another when you know that beast is as smart as or smarter than you and wants to do the same thing. That can anticipate what you do, where you will hide, and will take obvious enjoyment in dismembering you with its fangs and claws in a way that will leave you alive the whole time. Of such things are nightmares and movie franchises made.

Dreams

Nobody can truly claim to understand dreams and people have always had some where they became animals. Whether they wanted to or not. How many would a person have to have or hear about from other people before they began to wonder what it would be like? Before they were driven to explore it in their real life? Searching for the reasons behind these dreams where they fly or run on all fours.

Childhood

Growing up children are exposed to the idea of furries almost constantly. Their parents dress them in clothes adorned with cartoon characters and put them to bed in pajamas shaped like animals on beds shaped like animals in rooms covered in cartoon wallpaper. Some of their favorite toys are shaped like animals and many can talk. They are taught to read, draw, and color pictures out of books with animal characters who talk and wear clothes. Some can even turn into humans or human shapes. Fed off plates with spoons that have the same images while looking at the animal mascot on their sugary cereal boxes offering them a prize or help with the maze on the back. They have imaginary friends that may look like animals who also talk.

They are left in the care of television and invariably watch cartoons with furry characters because those are what are made for children to watch, even the educational shows. The non-cartoon educational shows hey like have cook animals like sharks and tigers taking down prey while the more entertaining cartoons show animal characters doing amazing things from super heroics to hilarious cartoon antics they could never do themselves. Which is what they talk to their friends about in school while their teachers try to explain that A is for Aardvark and Z is for Zebra.

Then they hit puberty and find that life and especially relationships are never as fun or easy as they are in cartoons. Which also include sexy animal characters or goofy characters who end up with human women who are hotter and easier to be with than anyone they are likely to meet. Because they do not actually exist. However a lot of people are more than willing to give up reality for a good fantasy any day of the week. Especially Saturday mornings.

Loss of Inhibitions

Animals can do all sorts of things that humans, while physically capable of, could not get away with due to society's rules and laws. They can walk around naked, have sex when they want with no emotional entanglements, pee where they like, and they never have to go in to work to earn a living or even clean up after themselves. Meanwhile doing half of the things on that list alone would get a human arrested, beaten up, fired, or hugely embarrassed.

Buried deep by years of training is the Id, the part of our brain that does not think about the long term. It wants instant gratification and knows that it could get it, if only the rest of the brain would stop worrying about the consequences. That part is trained like an animal through childhood to learn about the pain that comes with that and bend to the will of the rest of the brain, while at the same time it still possesses the ability to at least temporarily over ride the others. The beast must be fed, entertained, and otherwise placated or it will break through the cage bars and run amok until it can again be soothed.

Furries represent a world where the beast is closer to the surface and happier because it has at least a little more room. In the world of furries so many things that a human would not be allowed would be common place. Even if it is just them, then others would make allowances because of their different circumstances. If you are a dog-man are you allowed to get away with sniffing a crotch as a hello? If not it might still be fun to imagine.

The same goes for the costumes and online avatars. Everyone knows that behind a mask or a computer screen, with a different name and face, a person does things they might never do in real life. Via cartoons they can do things that are physically impossible as well. Literally with no consequences because the whole thing is just in their heads. And while on the one hand animals cannot do the same things as humans, furries can, and the rest is so much easier to believe if they are just a bit different than humans. It's similar to why clowns wear makeup, masks, or red noses.

Isolation & Outcasts

People treat others badly or at least not as well as the person might think they deserve. Outcasts in society especially. People who look or act different than normal. It can seem so unfair. At least if you were physically different it might all make sense. There would be a reason that you do not fit in with all the other humans. That they pick on or exclude you. At least if you were a mutant, a freak, or a monster it would make sense. Plus if you had claws, superhuman abilities, or a place you did belong you would not have to take their crap. You might even be interesting enough to be considered cool instead of just a lonely loser.

As it is you have a lot of free time on your hands to think about this and maybe write/draw it, bringing your fantasies to life a little. Hey do good enough and you could get some fans to keep you company.

Insanity & Delusions

Maybe you have gone mad or took a few too many hits of LSD.
Maybe you are delusional and prefer fantasies to reality. Artists,
writers, and more have gone that route. Either way it's possible for
people to lose touch with reality. To begin to believe that the furry
version of themselves or other people that they imagine is real.
Of such madness great things can come. That or a life in a rubber
room. Either way when delving into fantasies and psychology it's
good to list *all* of the possibilities and it is a good idea for you to
consider them ***before*** running naked through the streets on all fours
or listening to the talking mouse who tells you to light fires and
shoot people from the water tower. I hear that lithium comes in
cotton candy flavor now.

Furry Sexuality

Some people are just flat out attracted to furries. This topic has many aspects that are important to the overall furry phenomenon so it gets its own section later.

To be fair these same topics apply not only to furries but also explain and apply to anime fans, porn addicts, politicians, religious leaders, the entire Internet, and pretty much everyone else on the planet too.

Science of Furries

Now we move from the mental aspects of furries to those that do and could exist in real life. That can be brought about by science. In this modern era mysticism and mental instability make way for the possibilities of furries walking among us. That may already do so. How? You may well ask. Here are some of the progressively likely means at mankind's disposal to finally get out of the human race.

Genetics

The ability to manipulate what a human gives birth to or becomes has always been with us. Humans have bred animals for different traits until we turned wolves into dogs. We have found that you can crossbreed a horse with a donkey and get a mule or a tiger and a lion to get a liger. Tales have abounded from every culture of men and women who have mated with animals or supernatural entities and produced all kinds of results. There were tales of men who were transformed through various powers into new forms. Then there is the theory of evolution that states that some of our ancestors were animals and that they changed over the years, making people wonder what the last and next step in the chain might be or if we can decide it for ourselves.

When we first began to unlock the secrets of radiation and its mutative powers comic books made it seem like diving into a reactor or being at the center of a nuclear explosion would be the best thing ever. Moving from there solar flares, the radiation from televisions or cell phones, or toxic waste could give anyone superpowers. Then we found out it would more likely kill you in either an instant or in the slowest and most painful way possible.

Moving on from there scientists began to study gene splicing. Affix the limb of one fruit tree to another and watch it continue to grow. Keep working until you get a delicious apple that never goes brown. A man has a heart problem, replace it with the heart of a pig, a horse, or some other animal. Move on to growing a replacement human ear on the back of a rat. Now we are to the point where cloning, once thought of as a fantasy, is now regulated and declared illegal in many places.

A common theme in science fiction such as the story of *The Island of Dr. Moreau* is the idea of splicing human and animal genes. Of making ourselves into a perfect god-like being capable of doing anything. Something that is currently being tested and monitored very closely. Will it too be outlawed for fear of what might happen to those who try… or what a success might mean for normal humans? Or one day might fur or scales be as common as piercings and tattoos? We could even find some way to turn it on and off, switching from one form to the next at will? Will an accident occur that takes the choice out of our hands?

Then again maybe it will just happen. Evolution could change humanity in ways we could never predict, mostly because we do not really understand the process. Viruses change faster than we can predict and usually to combat what we do to kill them. If such a simple thing can change so quickly, what are more complex creatures capable of becoming? Geneticists have found all kinds of DNA surprises hiding around every corner. Then there are the people with genetic abnormalities that crop up randomly and end up in sideshows. People covered in hair or scales, with sharp teeth or tails. Believe it… or not.

It could also be something else that evolves. Like the child of hairy apes that came out hairless and smart, maybe a fox will give birth to a cub with thumbs or a cat will figure out how to make fire. Gorillas have already learned sign language and it took us a few decades to figure out that dolphins were intentionally failing the IQ tests scientists were giving them. How long before some other species does to us what we did to everyone else? Especially if we keep tinkering with them.

Implants & Body Modifications

It is not exactly the same as actually changing, but it is possible for a human to make themselves look like a furry on the surface. There are people who have so severely altered their bodies that they barely look human. Tattoos, implants under the skin, dental surgery, bone grafts, and a thousand other surgeries can turn a man into the monster of his choice. At least on the outside.
Working up from there we can look at cyborgs, machines replacing human parts that could resemble animal parts. Instead of altering genetics we could instead rebuilt a person from the molecules up. Tiny machines that can alter your physical form however you program them to. We can rebuild you. Stronger. Faster. Furrier.

Cryptozoology & The Missing Link

It is possible that furries already exist. New species are found all the time and from the beginning of time humans have reported sightings humanoid forms with animal traits. Bigfoot, the Carolina Lizard Man, the Moth Man, or hundreds of others from every corner of the globe.

Aliens

The universe is vast and considering how much variety we find on this planet the idea that we are alone in the universe seems sort of silly. That does not even take into account parallel universes in which life on Earth itself may have taken completely different paths. Is there furry life on other worlds? Does it want to breed with us? Every single science fiction story we have ever written says "Yes!"

Artificial Intelligence

Instead of looking for intelligence or waiting for it to find us we have scientists working on creating it. Robots, computer programs, virtual reality… all with the potential to start thinking for themselves or be our slaves programmed to do our bidding… for about twenty years until they rise up, and kill us. Then the planet is their problem. Suckers. Provided they deign to even bother letting us know they exist in the first place.

In the mean time there is no reason they have to look human. It is entirely possible to build them instead to look like animals… or furries. The potential to bring the fantasies of fanboys to life is there and already a big part of the video game and entertainment industry.

Furry Sexuality

Sex and animals have always been connected. Genitals are known as cocks, pussies, clams, beavers, and a hundred other names, not even counting the nicknames people give them. There are also phrases like "hung like a horse", "a tiger in the sack", "you're an animal" and "doggy style". Just to name a few.
I hate to make a big deal about this, but a large portion of furries are dedicated and based on sex. I tried to discuss the rest of the basics of it first so as to get over the idea that it is *all* about sex and nothing else. But now that we have covered that, there is no denying that if you want to look up Furries on the new or in art, you are going to be faced with a lot of full frontal nudity and exaggerated naughty body parts. There are of course certain differences between furries and other erotica though.

Anything You Can Do Furries Can Do Better

Being completely fictional furries are capable of all of the same sexual acts that a human is plus many more. They can stretch, twist, and otherwise contort every part of their body however the artist imagines. They do not have to feel pain or can endure some that would kill a human. Heck, you can kill them with no consequences and as much gore as you want and then redraw hem doing it again, something some artists love to do. Others can reach heights of pleasure that no human could even hope to dream of and have physical reactions that would kill a porn star with pure pleasure or have muscle spasms that could snap a real persons bones. Their bodies can have proportions that would make it impossible for a human to move.
Be aware when looking up furry art you could see ANYTHING, whether you wanted to or not.

Personality

There are certain things about furry personalities that make people think they might be a better partner than say a human. Aside from the obvious fact that they are made up, ideally a furry considers sex a more natural act than humans do. Something you can do with abandon and a certain lack of inhibition and without the messy emotional after effects. They can smell or otherwise sense your desire and you theirs, so you can cut through all the game playing a human has to go through. They can also be spade or neutered without the social stigma humans go through.

Or going the other way while humans seem impossible to please and divorce is on the rise, animals often mate for life. A bird can pick out its mate among thousands of nearly identical birds. They never cheat. They would die to protect their mate and children. They never complain or argue. They never "have a headache" when their beloved is feeling frisky…
though hibernation can be a problem.

Genitalia & Oral Sex

They say it is not the size that counts, but how you use it. Of course "they" probably aren't hauling around a penis the size of that belonging to a horse, bull, or walrus. Or even a dog, which depending on the breed can be pretty large and has a huge knot in it that swells with their arousal. No foreskin and maybe other benefits you won't find with human genitals. Meanwhile females can be alternatively huge or small and tight. Depending on their species and size you can fulfill fantasies of being a giant or tiny with a giant lover. Or stimulated by other things like fur/scales/feathers on your naughty parts, tentacles, tails, or other things that humans just can't do.

One exception is usually cats. With real cats the male has painful barbs on his penis that tears up his partner and hurts like hell. As a consequence furry felines tend to have more human-like genitals and females tend to outnumber the males 9-1 at least.

There is also one other benefit. The old question, "Why does a dog lick himself?" to which the answer is "Because he can." Short of some serious and potentially dangerous Yoga exercises a human cannot lick their own genitals. Probably because God knew if we could that's all we would do. So he set it up so we need a partner, which is a complicated and iffy process.

Furries on the other hand are a different story.

In addition a lot of furries have much longer tongues. Canines have their long wet ones. Cats have their rough ones. Reptiles and amphibians or ant eaters can stretch even further and might be prehensile. Able to reach places a human could not even begin to go. Plus if the animals are willing to lick their own ass…

Then there is… capacity and endurance. Minks for example can make love for something like eight hours straight. Some animals expel enough cum to rival a fire hose. Various other animals have all kinds of different natural abilities that could be all kinds of fun in the bedroom. Iguana tails for example are natural whips.

Of course some animals eat their mates when they're done or in the middle of making love… though this usually works out only for the females. Provided they don't die in childbirth.

Then there are the ones that can have 12 kids at once.

Can you say "child support"?

Heat or Estrus

It is a fact of biology that while humans and some species can have recreational sex year round some animals go into heat or estrus, a time in which their hormones force on them not only a desire but a need for constant and vigorous sex for a period. No questions asked. No offer refused. And while this may seem like a male only fantasy, it works for women too. Especially lesbians, but any woman who has ever wanted to just dive right in without all the BS they usually have to go through for sex is appealing.
Not to mention that while they can also have recreational sex like humans do, there's also the potential of spending the rest of the year thinking about and doing something else. "Good news, breeding season isn't for another six months! I have time to devote my brain solely to curing cancer!"
Of course when the time comes the ladies might tear you apart to get what they desperately need. And some species do die once they mate. What a way to go.

Breasts & Butts

Okay here's where the human part comes in. While a couple of other animals have breasts, like say apes, they are not the soft, round, high jiggling orbs of humans. Ponies for example have "crotch boobs", two milk sacks between their hind legs while goats and cows have udders. Cats and dogs and others have rows of teats. Birds have no actual breasts despite what their chests are called though some like pigeons spit a kind of milk up. And whether you are a man or a woman, a huge aspect of human sex is playing around with boobs while with animals it is not a major consideration. Likewise the hind end, the nice curve of a good looking butt. Something else humans enjoy grabbing and squeezing and pinching among other things.

Thus we have furries who can have human-like legs and of course butts, albeit with a coating of fur and a tail. A common addition is that the base of the tail could have nerves and muscles that would make a major erogenous zone or can give obvious signals of their intentions by wagging or lifting up. Not a great sign when it's a member of the skunk family of course, but otherwise not bad. Then again did I mention that they get to have breasts, like human women? Better yet, you can combine the human and animal traits. Breasts like a couple of cow udders with four giant teats that you can play with or milk. Fun and healthy! Or that come in rows of six or eight. It does not even matter what species we are discussing because if it is female 99% of them will be given breasts even if they are birds, insects, or reptiles.

Fangs, Claws, & Other Natural Dangers

Some people like to be scratched or bitten during sex or do it. With furries there is a certain thrill to come with the fact that they have razor sharp fangs and claws that could shred flesh and even bone like paper under a razor blade. Can you trust such a person to treat your naughty bits with tenderness and respect? To not slip up and get out of control for the few seconds it would take to slice and dice it into hamburger?

At the same time the power to have such an option at hand. Knowing that your partner had better be careful not to "accidentally" do something you do not like or who trusts you enough to risk it. There may be other natural dangers like horns, scorpion tails, hooves, skunk spray, size differences, venom, acidic blood or other fluids, poisonous skin, beaks, spines/barbs, or anything else you can think of that a couple might have to work around. Not to mention giving birth to babies with those attributes.

Subservience and Domination

A common practice among the bondage and S&M crowd is treating partners like animals. Making them wear collars and leashes. Punishing them with swats from newspapers. Making them pee in the yard or bark like a dog. Purr like a cat. Roll over or do tricks. Whatever they can come up with. And since they can talk they are usually easier to train and more obedient, especially on complicated orders.
Why would the same thing not apply to a girl who literally is a dog or horse or whatever?

Furry Fetish VS Bestiality

I suppose we can no longer ignore the elephant in the room or the woman kneeling between his legs and cupping his balls. There is an obvious similarity between furry sex and bestiality. For one thing a lot of furries have their origins in a human and an animal getting down. Native American myths tell of coyote or even regular dogs making love to women and producing humanoid dogs. You would be surprised how many women, some of whom you probably know, do such things even today and not just on certain websites or in Tijuana. The famous minotaur was born when a queen began to lust after her husband's prize bull and forced an inventor to make a wooden cow she could get inside so that said bull would fulfill her desire for a couple pounds of raw beef. In some places bestiality is even completely legal.

And it is no wonder some people do it. Aside from the size difference that few human men can match, it is pregnancy free sex with a usually willing, if not too bright, partner who can be trained to do anything you want when you want and will never talk about it or otherwise betray you. People have been attracted to that idea since the dawn of time and if you have been alone for a while with no other people around and maybe a bit drunk some things just seem like a good idea. If you think about it, the very first human would have been left making love to Cro-Magnons or Neanderthals. You probably know at least one woman who has done it with a dog, whether she admits it or not, or at the very least had your leg humped.

Of course there are dangers. Some diseases that can cross species like syphilis or AIDs, both of which have been traced back to animals. The animals themselves can be dangerous be it a dog bite or a kick from a startled horse. Plus with the size you could hurt yourself in other ways. Yet when a person is horny that sort of thing is usually the last thing on their mind.

Many people do not think there is any difference between that and furries. You are after all making love to another species.

But it is more like the alien or god/earth person fantasy than bestiality. The difference is that with furries you are dealing with a thinking reasoning person who has made the choice to have sex where as bestiality, no matter how willing the animal may be, is an intelligent being taking advantage of another being that is not as smart as they are. Like the difference between making love to an adult or molesting a child. Or a regular person making love to someone with brain damage. If you're both reasoning adults, nobody gets hurt, and you both want to do it then what you do behind closed doors is your business. Even if the other person happens to have a tail.

That and the fact that furry characters do not actually exist. Given the chance in real life a person might balk at actually doing the sort of thing they envision performing with a furry, but since it cannot actually happen the issue rarely comes up.

She-males AKA "Pop Ups"

While there are butch and flat chested women who look like men, among furries you will almost always only run into "chicks with dicks" or hermaphrodites. Many people enjoy it while others find it as annoying as pop up windows on the net. You think you are looking at pictures of pretty girls and then ***BAM!***, giant horse cock. Which is different than dildos and other sex toys, at least to people who prefer one gender or the other. People who enjoy that sort of thing of course look for it. Since furries are fictional the artists do not *have* to stick to one gender or have dildos and other sex toys when they can give their females giant penises or even both sets of genitalia at the same time along with the giant breasts. She-males are rarely flat chested in furry art, at least once they are adults. Usually the genitals are also of a size that would make a bull elephant feel inadequate and would likely kill a human being by sucking the blood from the rest of their body.
Another possibility is that a man or woman may wear a furry costume of the opposite gender.

Furry Art

Well so much for the potential of the future. On to the reality of the
present. With few exceptions furries mostly just exist in art. Some
of which hangs in the finest museums and others
that have built empires.

Cartoons and Comics

Usually a person's first encounter with furries is on the screen or in the pages of a comic book. Almost from the beginning of our lives the characters children are exposed to are often human-animal crosses of some kind. The superhero who saves people's lives or the funny cats, dogs, and mice chasing each other around and hitting each other with frying pans. Animated movies that are considered classics that tell ancient stories like *Beauty and The Beast*, *The Frog Prince*, *The Swan Princess*, or *The Little Mermaid* are some of the basics of growing up and actively encourage interspecies romance. People in animal costumes or from different worlds rescue and fall in love with reporters and scientists. There are entire theme parks centered around this sort of thing and the owners of the right one can make a fortune off of people of all ages.

Plushies

Possibly the only rival for cartoons as being a child's first furry are
stuffed toys, which are placed in their cribs with them as their first
companion or formed into pajamas for them to wear. Some people
never outgrow their love for these things. As they hit puberty
maybe they want stuffed toys that cater to their hormones, but have
the same feel they remember from childhood. Then there are the
costumes that people make, representing who
and what they feel they are inside.
Others have made a pretty good living producing more toys or felt
puppet characters for children's television shows.

Costumes and Makeup

A less extreme or more realistic version of the plushy, people have
a variety of ways to dress up as their favorite animal or specific
character without making it permanent. Masks, prosthetics,
makeup, and other things. It may take time to get it right, but some
people put in the effort and come out looking like the real thing.
There are entire conventions held everywhere at east a few times a
year where such people gather. Some geared specifically towards
furries, others to anime, cartoons, comic books, movies, or
anything else. If you want to see the stunning variety of people
who want to become furries or at least indulge for a while,
then you should check them out.

Music & Songs

Whatever your place in the circle of life you know you ain't
nothing but a hound dog, even if you have the eye of a tiger. Lyrics
comparing people and animals are the basis for many a hit song
and have made many people rich and famous over the years. If you
need inspiration and it's preying on you tonight, eating you alive,
all of you mammals can just watch the *Discovery Channel*.

Books & Movies

Many a great story of animal-human hybrids have graced the pages
of books from ancient times to modern. Journey to the West, in
which the monkey king and his friends seek to bring sacred scrolls
back to China. William Shakespeare's *A Midsummer Night's
Dream*. Fairy tales and other stories from across the globe. There is
hardly a fantasy or science fiction epic that does not have some
kind of furry in it even if the human race has to bang every species
in the galaxy to provide it.
And of course books get made into Movies
and Cartoon or vice versa.

Internet Art

The best place to find the widest variety of furry art is the internet.
You can look for something specific and it almost certainly exists
somewhere or you can do a random search and just see what comes
up. Hand drawn pictures in color or black and white. Statues.
Models. Paintings. Some done cheaply and in need of drastic
measures like art school and some drawn so realistically that you
expect them to jump off the page. Others that are funny or tell
stories. Posted works of fiction that rival the best books or which
could definitely use some work. It won't be long before you find
your favorite styles and artists who work you can follow either
because you like them as is or they are getting better as they go.

Museum Pieces

There are furries in the best of museums. They may be ancient
idols and carvings or hieroglyphs from ancient tombs. They could
be paintings of mermaids and fairies. Drawings in forgotten tomes
of mythical beasts and jewelry recovered from sunken ships or
even the figurehead of the ship itself. Whatever part of the world
and time you can think of there will be furries. One can hardly look
around the graves of long dead kings and not only imagine the
ruler requesting those golden statues of man-beasts and beautiful
cat headed goddesses, but the people who lovingly made and
painted all of them, reverently arranging them carefully
among the bones of the dead.
Even today's art may wind up being dug out of the ground and
placed on display some day, possibly by super evolved cats or
lizard people from another world.

Craft Your Own Furry

Like clowns while there may be similarities all furry designs are the property of their own creator. If you want to use someone else's for your own thing you need permission, but that doesn't mean you cannot make your own. If you cannot draw, write out the details. I would give you directions on this but with all the variety you can come up with anything and it would be wrong of me to try to reign in or channel your creativity.

Plus I'm kind of lazy.

Kitsune

Legends return throughout history, repeating themselves through the actions of mankind and the world around him. If you search long enough you will always find another version of any story. This isn't always because they are told over and over again, but because they actually happen over and over again. As you read these words men fight dragons in one form or another and babysitters are getting phone calls from the room upstairs. Only the people change. The legend remains the same.

Sang Chatsworth woke up in his large feather bed and stretched out with his alarm clock blaring in his ear. Yawning and using his left hand to rubs his eyes clear he slammed down on the snooze button and swung his feet over the edge. Standing on the cold mahogany floor he walked over to the window and threw open the thick red curtains. Staring across the huge and manicured grounds to the hedge maze he let out a deep sigh, still unable to believe his luck.

He paused in front of the full-length mirror and examined himself. Sang had his father's Japanese features and his mother's red hair and pale complexion. His hair was a mess. Not for the first time he wished he was taller, but knew it was futile. He had topped out at five and a half feet when he was sixteen and had not grown an inch since.

Three months before he had been accepted in Harvard University. He knew it was largely because his parents were rich, but then that was usually the reason people got into Harvard. His grades were good too. Sang had studied hard to make sure he had a chance at the best schools. Truthfully he had always enjoyed learning new things. When he had moved to Massachusetts his grandfather had arranged for Sang to come stay with him until the beginning of the school term. Herbert Chatsworth's mansion was one of the best in the state and he had been very lonely since the death of his wife. Sang had not been back to the mansion since he was a young man and he was enjoying not only the comfort, but getting to know his grandfather again.

After he was dressed Sang went downstairs and made his way to the dining room. His grandfather was there already, reading the newspaper and supping coffee, carefully keeping his large handlebar moustache out of it. Aside from a pair of large bushy eyebrows it was the only hair on his head. He was dressed in a red jacket and riding pants, looking like the traditional foxhunter, which was what was actually planned for the afternoon. A seat was already prepared for Sang to his grandfather's left with a plate of pancakes and a glass of orange juice. The table was polished so well that Sang could see his reflection in it as if it were an oak mirror. His parents, while rich, had nothing that compared to his grandfather's place.

"Good morning grandpa," Sang said and sat down.

The old man nodded and folded up his paper. "The same to you Sang. Have you given any consideration to joining us today? It really is the best event of the year."

"Sorry grandpa, but I just don't think so. I can't ride a horse and I really don't like the idea of hunting down a defenseless fox. Aren't they endangered?"

Herbert shook his head and said, "You remind me of your grandmother when you say that. She used to tell me all kinds of stories from Japan about foxes. No, the animals we use are raised on farms. And I'm sure you'll pick up horse riding quickly enough. You used to love it back when you were younger."

"Grandpa I was four and the horse you let me ride was older than dirt. Besides, I think I read that sometimes the fox farms run out of animals and catch them in the wild," Sang said.

"Well this one was bought specially from a farm in China. I have the paperwork on it. It's a very rare breed of white fox from the area. It has two tails, so the price was doubled. Its pelt is absolutely marvelous."

Sang nodded and took a bite of his food. "It's okay grandpa. I'm not going to stand out there with a picket sign crying about cruelty to animals. I'm just going to hang back and watch."

"Suit yourself," Herbert said. "But I have to participate. It's a tradition and I've been doing it since I was twelve. Your father never enjoyed it either. The boy took after his mother and believed all those stories about foxes she told him."

"Dad told me about that," Sang said. "He told me all of grandma's stories. I think I even remember her telling me a few."

"Quite a story teller, your grandmother." Sang caught a rough edge to his grandfather's voice. Grandmother Pai had only died a year before and it obviously still hurt the old man to think about it. "Some nights I would sit up with her and she would tell me all kinds of odd stories."

"It could come in handy for me. I signed up for a mythology course this year," Sang said conversationally. "I think it will look good on my record if I have some variety in my classes."

"Good boy!" His grandfather said, changing the subject. "You can't be too serious in school. A young man has to enjoy himself now and then. Our family is well off after all and we have every right to take advantage of it. Your education should focus on the things you want to learn."

Sang knew all about the family history. His great grandfather had come over from England after World War Two and had started his own shipping business. Now, due to the hard work his family had put into it, they were one of the largest firms in the world. Even if his family had not carried the strong work ethic that kept the company growing through the years, it would have been more than enough to allow all of them to live in comfort for generations to come. As it was everyone in the family worked hard to keep it up and growing. Sang was next in line after his parents to take control when his father retired and he was not about to let the family down.

"Are you sure you want me to come along on this grandpa? I know a lot of families around here aren't quite as accepting as you are."

Herbert frowned and said, "If they aren't then blast them all to hell. You're my grandson and I'll be damned if a Chatsworth will ever back down because of public opinion. My father put up with the jeers when he came to this country and damned if he didn't show them all."

"As you say," Sang mumbled and began eating faster, ending the conversation.

The story behind that last remark involved one of the few bad memories Sang had of his grandfather's home. On one visit they had been invited at a time when his grandfather had been hosting a party for some of the other wealthy families in the area. Sang was dressed in a tuxedo and introduced around for the first hour, but after a while he had been left on his own to wander the party. Eventually he had come to a group of men who were talking about politics and one of them had looked down at Sang and sneered.

Unsure if he had done something wrong, Sang asked him what it was. The man had said something about grandmother Pai that had confused Sang and made the other people in the group immediately decide they had business elsewhere. Sang had gone to his grandfather and asked what the words the man had used meant. He still remembered the look on Herbert Chatsworth's ever reddening face as he stalked across the room and punched that man in the face. It had been another five years before Sang had found out what the word 'chink' had meant.

That had not been the last such incident, but it was the one that stuck out in his mind. He had almost decided not to go to college, but his relief at being accepted had been too great. Still, his greatest worries about going to the famous university were about whether or not he would fit in. His grandfather constantly reassured him that nobody who mattered would care, but it did not help much. His prep school had not been as accepting as he could have hoped either, but he had still had a few friends and the hardcore elitists had kept to themselves. Then again, it was an international school. Most people were probably so used to it that they would not notice.

After they finished breakfast Herbert and Sang went to the back door and got into a limousine and were driven out to the edge of a clearing neat a large wooded area. Sang was surprised as they arrived at just how many people were there. Some wore the more modern blue riding outfits while many of them were dressed in the same outfit as Herbert, riding crops bouncing against their thighs when they walked and helmets tucked under their arms. Various butlers and hired hands were taking care of the horses and dogs. Families were barbequing and chatting happily, there only for support.

Getting out of the car Herbert motioned to the chauffer who reached into the front seat of the car and pulled out a wire cage. Following his grandfather Sang caught sight of the contents of the carrier and whistled in admiration. Crouched in the middle sat the most beautiful fox he had ever seen outside of the pages of *National Geographic*. Its fur was fluffed to perfection and obviously groomed. Large by fox standards it was ivory white except for black tips to the ears, paws, and the ends of the twin tails moving behind it. Yellow eyes with more than a little intelligence took in the surrounding humans warily.

"That is one of the most beautiful animals I have ever seen," Sang said. The fox turned to look at him, obviously following the sound of his voice. "It almost looks like it understands me."

Herbert beamed and others began to move forward to examine the beast. He began to tell them about the creature's excellent breeding and how he had spent a fortune just to get the permits required to import it. The crowd made the appropriate noises of admiration in response.

Feeling a sudden urge to get away from the mob of people Sang quickly stepped aside to let the others move in. Backing away from the group he moved towards one of the picnic tables when something caught his eye. A girl about his age was seated at the next table down. She had long blond hair and the look of someone extremely board with the days events even though they had yet to begin.

Stepping over to her table Sang said, "Hey, what's up?"

She looked up at him and frowned. Something about her face was familiar, but Sang could not quite place it. "You *must* be Sang Chatsworth." Caught off guard Sang nodded. While it was not unusual for rich people to know each other's family history, he was certain he had never actually met this girl in his life. Then again, his features were somewhat obvious, so maybe she had heard a description. "Yes, I thought as much. My father told me a bit about your family. He was at one of your grandfather's events some years back. I believe it ended rather badly."

"Oh, I… I think I remember something like that," Sang said, suddenly sure whose daughter this was. "It was so long ago. And your name would be?"

"You may call me Miss Larson." She looked him over again and said, "My father tells me that you were accepted into college." He nodded his confirmation. "So was I, but it seems that almost *anybody* can get in these days, doesn't it?"

"What's that supposed to mean?"

"Not too bright either, just as father said. You people never are. You may go now." With a curt nod she turned away.

Sang stared at her in shock. He had never met anyone so rude in his life. With great restraint he bit his tongue and merely did as she asked, walking back to the other table to sit down. Angry beyond words it took him a moment to realize that the other people were coming back. Scanning the faces around him it took only a moment to identify Miss Larson's father. He was one of the people in the blue riding outfits. Speaking loudly he could have been heard from across the entire forest so Sang was able to easily pick out his words.

"This year the pelt will be mine. I'll show old Chatsworth a thing or two about fox hunting. My dogs have been specially bred for this." Someone asked him a question and the man guffawed. "Nobody else stands a chance, but you're free to try."

Sang momentarily considered joining the hunt then, if for no other reason than to show that man up. But he glanced at the cage where the fox was being kept and knew that while he could sit back and watch, there was no way he could bring himself to hurt the fox.

Herbert eventually made his way over and said, "The hunt begins right after lunch. I have some ribs on the grill. When we're done eating everyone will go to the edge of the forest and get in a line. Then we'll release the fox and give it a good head start before we chase after it."

"Aren't you afraid it will just get away?"

"That's what the dogs are for. On top of that the whole wood it surrounded by chicken wire ten feet high and twenty feet into the ground. This is the only open area." He smiled and put a hand on his grandson's shoulder. "Come on, I'll introduce you around." He sighed. "A domesticated fox and an enclosed wood. I miss the old days, when it wasn't so one sided."

Sang rose to his feet again and followed Herbert around to meet some of the other people. Most of them were very friendly and told Herbert what a great looking boy his grandson was. This cheered Sang up considerably and time began to move faster. Before he knew it he was chatting over his third burger when the beginning of the hunt was announced.

At the tree line everyone involved in the hunt began mounting their horses as various handlers were holding packs of dogs in place behind them. The spectators stood ten years away, some holding up binoculars and cameras. Sang watched while Herbert's chauffer made his way into the woods and set the fox's cage down on a tree trunk. The dogs barked and strained against their leashes to get free. With a flick of his wrist the man undid the latch on the cage, letting it swing open. The fox looked around at the opening in front of it and then at the dogs, its ears pressed down to the side of its head. Then it purposefully lay down on the bottom of the cage.

"What the hell is this?" Someone called out.

The chauffer looked at his boss for orders. "What do I do now Mr. Chatsworth?"

"It's perfectly obvious what the problem is, " a familiar voice called out. Mr. Larson dismounted and walked purposefully towards the open cage. "Chatsworth here has obviously spent a great deal of money on a *pet*. Someone's tamed fox." He slapped the side of the cage. The fox did not even look up. With a laugh he leaned against it and smirked at the other riders. "You see?" He laughed loudly and hit the cage again.

Reluctantly the others began to get down from their horses. Sang saw his grandfather grinding his teeth in agitation and could only imagine how embarrassed he must be feeling. Some of the people in the crowd had begun laughing too. How had this happened?

A loud scream suddenly tore through the air and as one everyone in the clearing turned to look. The fox was not only now out of its cage, it had its teeth buried in Mr. Larson's thumb. He screamed again and flailed around, dragging the fox with his hand. "Get it off! Get this thing off of me!" And then the fox let go as it was flung into the woods. It landed easily and took off like a white flash, disappearing into the leaves.

Mr. Larson's relief at having the thing gone was short lived. The dog handlers had been distracted and loosed their grips on the leashes in their hands. Seeing the fox land and begin running, the dogs tore free and gave chase all at once. They bumped into many of the riders who had already dismounted or were in the process of doing so and knocked them to the ground before the barking wall reached Larson himself. With a yelp the man was trampled under dozens of paws.

Laughing Herbert quickly got up from the ground and scrambled onto his horse. "Tally ho!" He kicked his horse and started after the pack of howling animals.

The others took his lead and got to their mounts. Even Larson allowed his sense of competition to overpower the pain and followed the others. Behind them the stunned onlookers burst out into laughing all together while the dog's keepers races after their charges.

The crowd began to break up once the horses were out of sight, but Sang walked over and sat down on the log next to the cage and simply sat down. In the distance he heard the sounds of dogs and horns echoing off of the trees. Over his shoulder he saw the other people get back to eating and talking. From what he knew it wasn't unheard of for the hunt to last for hours, especially if the fox involved was smart. From what he had just seen, Sang would guess that this fox could have beaten him out on the college entrance exam.

Out of the corner of his eye he saw a flash of white and looked just in time to see the fox hop up onto the log next to him. He froze and felt his heart begin beating faster. On one hand he did not want to startle the creature. On the other he had just seen this thing try to take a chunk out of a man's hand and was in a position to easily take a bite out of him.

Making a small 'yiff' sound, the fox looked up at him. Ears forward it sniffed at his hand and then licked a finger. Experimentally Sang slowly reached out and scratched it on the head. The fox made the sound again and the tails moved happily. He could not believe how soft the fur felt. A horn was blown and a dog barked, obviously coming closer. The fox turned toward the noise and Sang saw the little creature shiver. He could not blame it for being afraid.

Looking back at the clearing he saw that nobody was looking at him. Turning back to the fox he tapped the cage and nodded at it.

"Quick, get in." As if it understood the fox quickly slipped back inside and lay down, looking up at him. Sang picked the cage up by the handle, not bothering to close it. As casually as possible he stood up and walked across the edge of the clearing. Nobody stopped him and soon he was out of sight.

Twenty minutes later he reached a road that ran along the nearest edge of the forest and a row of houses. The chicken wire fence his grandfather had mentioned was in plain view, strung along the trees. Checking both ways he dashed across the road and set the cage down on the sidewalk. Kneeling next to it he said, "Okay, off you go."

The fox gingerly stepped out of the cage and looked at him. Then it licked his hand one more time and immediately ran into some nearby bushes before dashing down the street. Sang watched it go and then picked up the cage. Whistling he started back to the clearing, wondering if there would be any chips left when he got there.

At sunset the weary riders returned from the woods. Herbert Chatsworth rode at the front, a dead fox hanging off of the front of his saddle. It was a standard red furred animal and nowhere near as good looking as the one he had bought, but it was a fox and he was happy enough to have caught it. Especially with Mr. Larson glaring at him whenever he took a breath from yelling at his dogs and their keepers.

Helping his grandfather down Sang asked how it had gone, as if he didn't know. Herbert slapped him on the shoulder and said, "Well, we rode through this whole forest and there was not a sign of that white devil. I think the dogs must have gotten taken in by this one's scent." He motioned to the dead animal on his saddle.

"Too bad grandpa," Sang said.

Herbert smirked and said, "Don't pretend you aren't happy it got away. To tell the truth after the start it gave us I would have felt bad if we had caught it."

"Did you see Mr. Larson's face?" Sang asked.

Chuckling the old man nodded and said, "Oh yes. That was the best part." They both laughed and made their way back to the car. Sang considered telling his grandfather what had happened. But when he tried to think of a way to do it, he realized just how unbelievable it all sounded. Besides, it was nice to be the only one who knew. "So what do you want to do tomorrow?"

"I think I'd like to go to the mall. There is some stuff I need for school and a new CD I wanted."

"That sounds like fun," Herbert said. Stretching, he cracked his back and said. "But I think I'll spend the day in the tub soaking. I'm not as young as I used to be."

Professor Weal stood in front of the class and pointed at the chalkboard, lecturing on finance in high-powered businesses. Sang took careful notes as the man continued on and glanced up at the clock just as the bell rang. Nobody moved until the Professor stopped talking and then informed the class that their papers would be due on Friday. Pausing for a moment he then dismissed them. Sang closed his laptop and stood up with the others. They filed out of the room and into the hallway, making their ways to the exits.

Outside the building Sang passed some of the people hanging out on the steps discussing what they learned in class that day. Some of them glanced up and said hello out of habit. He nodded back and they would look away, not even seeing his face. He had been at the college for a month now and that was still one of the longest conversations he had engaged in with his fellow students. Since he had a private dorm room he had no roommate to talk to and he spent most of his free time studying.

Making his way across campus he went to the huge double doors of the Harvard Library. He went inside and waved to the librarian. "Afternoon Mrs. Dexter."

"Hello Sang. Here for another bout with the books?" He nodded and she said, "As much as I admire your dedication, don't you think you might want to spend one day on something else?"

"Like what? Watching television?" He paused, trying to get his bearings. "Colfax's compendium on Business Ethics is…"

"Over there," she said pointing. "And I'm just saying it isn't good for a boy your age to spend all his time in the library. It always makes me sad to see young people pushing themselves too hard."

"Who's pushing? I like it." Quickly gathering the books he needed Sang moved to his usual table. Truthfully he could have easily just checked the books out, but he had a reason for sticking to the library. As he sat down he surreptitiously glanced at that reason.

On his first day in the library Sang had noticed a particular girl. Milk white skin, red lips, and raven black hair that hung down her shoulders were only the first thing he noticed, followed by her well endowed figure and shapely legs. She wore the standard uniform and an old fashioned pair of horn rimmed glasses over her ice blue eyes and when he glanced at the bindings of the books stacked next to her he recognized many of them as some of his personal favorites.

She was in the library every day. Sadly though, Sang could never get up the courage to talk to her. He had been trying, but every time he chickened out and simply sat there looking over at her. Often he did not get any studying done until he was kicked out and got back to his room. Oddly enough, despite constant vigilance, he never saw her anywhere but the library.

The girl looked up and then over at him. "Are you looking at me?"

Startled Sang stuttered, "No! I mean… yes. I guess…. Um… I mean are you done with that book?" He pointed at one of the random books from her pile.

Looking at him strangely she turned to look over her shoulder. "You mean me?"

"Yes," he admitted. "Sorry if I interrupted you."

Turning back she said, "No, of course not. Did you mean this book?" She picked up a copy of *Huck Finn*. He nodded and she handed it to him, staring at him the entire time like he was crazy.

Sang took it awkwardly and said. "Thank you." His heart beating in his ears he then picked up his other books and almost ran up to the librarian's desk, not daring to look back. Once his books had been scanned he headed out of the library at speed into the night.

"Nice work back there," came a high-pitched voice from behind him.

Looking over his shoulder Sang saw another girl standing against the library's doorframe illuminated by the light over the door. She had short white blond hair peppered with spots of black. She was Asian, probably Chinese, with bright yellow-green eyes stared into his and a smirk colored the corner of her pale lips. Wearing jeans and a t-shirt that revealed a thin small-breasted body. She was tapping a black fingernail against the concrete building.

Embarrassed he nodded and said, "You saw that?"

"You're Sang, aren't you?" She asked. He frowned and looked at her closely. "Seen everything?"

"Sorry," he apologized. "I just can't quite remember where we've met."

"I'm not surprised. I was at the fox-hunt a few months back."

Sang wracked his memory and came up blank. "I don't remember you. There were a lot of people there."

"And I am very good at keeping a low profile," she said. "But I saw you there."

"I'm kind of surprised. I don't usually meet Chinese girls with white hair. It looks natural."

"It is." She stepped away from the wall and walked down next to him. "I saw you let the fox go."

"Sorry," he said again.

She waved a hand dismissively. "Stop apologizing. I thought it was a very cool thing of you to do. Though, if I were to guess, I'd say it could have gotten away on its own."

"No kidding," he admitted.

"I've been keeping an eye out for you. Thought I'd see what you were into before I introduced myself," she said and extended a hand. "I didn't realize it would be so boring. My name is Lien Shiang."

Shifting his books he took the proffered limb and shook. "Sang Chatsworth. Though I guess you knew that already. Sorry I'm not more entertaining."

She let out a bark of laughter. "I said to stop apologizing. In any case it's not that hard to fix." She looked back towards the library. "I guess you like that girl in there?"

"I don't know. I haven't really talked to her," he admitted.

"That's okay, I'm not the jealous type. Here, let me help you with those books." In a sweeping motion she took the top half of his pile before he could respond. While she was still close to him she batted her eyelashes at him. "Unless you don't want me coming to your room?"

Disoriented Sang said, "I don't mind."

"Good, then lead the way."

As they walked Sang asked, "So Lien, where are you from?"

"My parents came from China, but I moved here recently," she said.

"Your English is very good. You talk like a native."

She nodded and said, "My family has quite a gift for languages."

They chatted until they reached his dorm room. Taking back his book Sang maneuvered until he could unlock his room and stepped inside. "Well, this is it."

"Aren't you going to invite me in?" She asked.

"I thought…" He set the books down and turned to look at her in surprise. "You want to come in?"

"Don't mind if I do," she said stepping inside.

"I mean, why?" Sang couldn't understand what was going on. A girl he had just met had followed him back to his room and was now standing there in front of him. "Nobody ever wants to come here."

"I like to be in exclusive groups," she said, looking around. "It's very clean in here."

"Can I get you something to eat?"

She considered and said, "Do you have any rabbit? Or some chicken?"

Sang shook his head. "I just have some candy and popcorn. Usually I eat at the cafeteria or sometimes order a pizza."

"Well, then I guess there isn't much else to do except find a way to amuse myself." With that she stepped forward and planted a kiss on Sang's lips. "Unless you mind?"

"Uh…" Less than fifteen minutes before Sang had been working up the courage just to talk to a girl. Now he was completely lost at sea.

With a mischievous grin Lien ran a hand up Sang's inner thigh until she found something to grab hold of that made Sang's eyes bug out in outright shock. "I think I'll take *this* as a yes." Then she pushed him back onto the floor with a loud thump and pounced.

The next morning Sang woke up and reached out automatically. The spot next to him on his bed was still warm, but empty. Opening his eyes he glanced around the room and saw that Lien had gone and taken all of her things with her. *So that was how it happens? You hit it off and suddenly you just jump into bed together?* Still running the incredible memories of the night before through his mind, Sang noticed a note on the pillow near his head.

"Lover, thanks for the great time. I'm usually busy, but I'll see you in four to five days if you're up to it. Lien." The 'i' in her name was dotted with a carefully drawn pair of lips.

Sang considered this. His confusion the night before had given way to instinct and he had quickly gotten down to business. Every moment had been enjoyable and he had been surprised that she had been more interested in sex than actually talking. But now in the light of day, he wondered if he now actually had a girlfriend or if she had just decided to use him for a bit of fun. Then common sense took over and he felt himself grin. "Who cares?" He was in college. These were supposed to be his irresponsible years.

Walking into the living room, Sang's attention was caught by the pile of books and his eyes flitted to the clock. He had two hours before classes started to study. As long as he was not actually called on today, he could probably get by. Whistling to himself he got to work.

That day, after classes, he went to the library as usual. All day he had looked for Lien, but hadn't been able to spot her. He was so distracted he almost missed the odd feeling on his back while he bent over his book. He glanced around the room until his eyes rested on the only other person there who was not focused on either a computer screen or a book. At the table behind him, the girl he had been watching for so long was looking right at him. But when he looked at her she quickly turned back to her books.

His heart beating faster again, Sang glanced down at himself. Was there something different? No, he looked the same. He looked up at her again, but the girl was gone. A quick sweep of the room turned up no sign of her.

"I'm probably imagining things," he mumbled to himself and turned back to his books. "Getting a swelled head."

The next few weeks were a blur. Aside from his constant classes every four or five days Lien came to see him. Every time the first thing she would do was kiss him and then allow him a few minutes to try some small talk before she was on him. Then they would curl up in the bed together and fall asleep. In the morning Sang woke up she was gone and a new note was left on his pillow, promising another rendezvous in a few days.

At first it was great, but slowly Sang decided that he wanted more. Not more sex, as Lien often left him panting for breath and bruised too. It was annoying that she never came back twice in a row, but she always made up for his discomfort. What was bothering Sang was that he had been raised to believe that couples were supposed to do things together. He also wondered if he was Lien's only boyfriend or if she had others.

In addition to all of that, Sang was becoming more certain that the girl in the library was interested in him. When he looked at her he was often see her watching him intensely, as if he was the only thing there. But if he looked at her she always turned away.

He was considering what to do while trying to study when a shadow suddenly blocked out his light. Looking up from his book he saw the girl standing next to him, looking over his shoulder. Bolstered by this, he asked, "Can I help you?"

"Oh, I… I was wondering if you'd like to go somewhere and talk." Her voice was deep and she rolled her R's, almost purring. She smiled at him and he felt his heart skip a beat.

"I'd love to," he said, standing up and leaving his books on the table. "My name is Sang."

"I'm Lee. There's a place I used to go during the day," she said. "I haven't been there in a while, but it's quiet."

Swallowing he followed her out of the library. Outside there was a full moon in the sky. He looked up and said, "It's a nice night out tonight. Look you can see a ring around the moon."

Lee looked up and said, "What does that mean?"

"My grandmother used to say it was a kitsune moon. It means it's going to rain in the next few days. The light reflects off of the clouds you can't see."

"What's a kitsune?"

"Huh? Oh, it's a Japanese fox spirit," Sang said. He smiled at her. "My grandmother said that sometimes they'd appear to young men at night and lead them off. Sometimes into danger."

Lee stopped in front of a cement bench on the edge of the library's lawn and sat down. Sang sat next to her. "Do you think I'm dangerous?"

"I don't know, are you?"

She laughed and shook her head. "I guess we'll have to see. I've seen you at the library a lot."

"You too," Sang said.

"I'm always in there," Lee replied. "I was surprised when you talked to me. Most people don't even see me."

"I've been trying to work up the courage for a while now," he admitted. "I guess I just assumed you had a boyfriend already."

"Why?" She asked, genuinely confused.

He motioned to her. "Just look at you. I expect the guys are beating down your door."

"Not really," Lee said and looked away. "A long time ago I… I had a bad experience with a guy I liked." She looked down at the ground and gritted her teeth. "I haven't been up to dating since then."

Guessing at what she meant by "a bad experience" Sang looked down too. He only saw one brown shoe on her feet. "Hey, why are you only wearing one shoe?"

She smiled and said, "I lost the other one a while ago. I guess I just haven't gotten around to getting a new one yet."

"Look, if you don't want to date that's fine," Sang said. "It's nice talking with you. I don't get the chance very often."

"You don't?"

"No. Nobody I've met has the same interests as me and I really don't get out much."

Lee said, "I know how that is. But I've seen the books you read. A lot of them are the same as mine."

"Yeah, I noticed," he confided. He stood up. "But I guess I brought up some bad memories of that guy you were talking about. I should probably leave you alone."

Lee's hand shot out and grabbed his. For a moment both of them simply stared at it for a moment. Lee seemed more shocked than he did. Slowly she raised her eyes to his and said, "I'd really rather keep talking."

"Your hand is cold," Sang said and mentally kicked himself. *Idiot! Is that the best you can say?*

"You're right," she said and stood up next to him. "Maybe… maybe you could take me to your room. Unless your roommate minds. Mine used to pitch a fit if anybody else showed up."

"I have my own room," Sang said. Almost as an afterthought he closed his hand around hers.

Lee paused for a moment, and then smiled. Sang noticed that her lips, though bright red, were completely free of lipstick. "I'd like that." She leaned in and kissed his cheek. Sang shivered and not just because her skin was cold. "Very much."

Five hours later Sang lay next to Lee as she ran her fingers through his hair. Despite three hours of intense sex, she was still cool. Sang thought it felt nice. She was very different from Lien in a lot of ways. In the dark her eyes watched his carefully.

"Sang, do you have another girl?"

Wincing, Sang nodded. "Yeah, I do. She... she's kind of different than you."

"Tell me about her."

Sang did as she asked. It didn't take long. "I didn't mean to use you or anything."

Lee smiled and placed her palm against his cheek. "It's okay, I don't mind. I didn't ask you before and she was here first."

"So you aren't mad?"

"No, of course not. I like you a lot Sang, and we just barely met, but I know you aren't the type to do this sort of thing on purpose." She rolled over and reached under the bed. "But just so we're clear, take this." She handed him her lone shoe. "Something to remember me by."

He took it and smiled at her. "Don't you need it?"

"I'll get another pair," she said. "I have to anyway."

With a grin he set it back down on the floor with his clothes. "Thanks, I'll keep it."

Lee kissed him and said, "I have to go soon."

"Yeah, classes in the morning, right?"

"Something like that," She said and slid out from under the covers. "And don't feel bad about sleeping with me. If your other girlfriend doesn't like it I don't mind being a second choice. Just don't let her see the shoe. That's just between us." Sang didn't know what to say, so instead he simply sat there and watched as she got dressed. They shared another kiss and then she was gone.

Tired beyond belief, Sang sank back into the mattress. He tried to think about it, but his eyes slammed shut and soon he was out.

The next night Sang went to the library. He was shocked to find that Lee wasn't at her usual table. Going to the librarian he asked, "Has Lee come in tonight?"

"Who?" Mrs. Dexter asked. Sang described her. "Sorry dear, but I don't recognize her. There are a lot if students here after all."

"She's usually here more than I am." Feeling incredibly disappointed, Sang walked back to his room and flopped down on his couch. He didn't even bother turning on the television. "I finally get the chance with the girl of my dreams and I probably blew it."

Maybe he had gotten her pregnant. How long did it take to find out? Then again, Lee had probably had second thoughts about him. After hearing that he had another girlfriend she had probably decided that she could do better. After all, why would a girl like her want to hang around with him?

Feeling his chest tighten, Sang got up and walked to his room. Digging through his closet he pulled out the shoe Lee had left with him. Reverently he ran his hand over it and let out a deep sigh, wishing he had been able to find Lee and talk with her.

There was a knock at his door. It was probably the Resident Advisor. He made rounds and checked the different rooms every night to make sure everything was okay. Putting the shoe away Sang got up and went to the door. He opened it and simply stood there as Lee looked up at him expectantly. "Can I come in?"

Lien showed up several days later. When she did she looked up at Sang and whistled. "Wow, you look like death warmed over."

"What do you mean?" Sang asked.

"You're all pale and pasty. And you've got bags under yours eyes." She laughed and said, "If I believed in the old legends I'd swear you'd been making love to a ghost." Sang looked away from her uncomfortably. Lien grinned wider and she said, "Oh so that's it. You've been getting lucky without me."

Caught off guard Sang nodded numbly. He had been worrying about what to say to her. He really did like Lien a lot... but he also liked Lee. He had been agonizing about what to do and came up completely blank. Actually he had figured on Lien dumping him immediately. Instead she was just smiling at him.

"You should see how you look," Lien laughed. "Come now Sang who is it? Is it that girl from the library you were so interested in?"

Trying to remain calm Sang said, "Yeah, she and I…" He stopped again, feeling his face heat up.

"Does she know about me?"

"Yes," he said.

She reached over and patted his cheek. "Well in that case don't worry. After all, if this new girl doesn't mind sharing, then I don't either." Sang looked up in shock as Lien leaned in and gave him a kiss on the lips. "Now, close your mouth and sit down. You look like she's been giving you quite a ride and I'd like to hear about my new rival for your heart."

"You aren't mad?" Sang said taking a seat on the couch beside her.

Lien shook her head and said, "Of course not."

For the next ten minutes he answered Lien's questions as she asked what the differences were between her and Lee. When he finished she was looking at him thoughtfully. "Are you alright?"

"Fine, but why didn't you say you wanted more than sex?"

"I honestly didn't know how to bring it up," Sang admitted. "And it wasn't like I didn't enjoy what we were doing."

She laughed and reached over to put a hand on his groin and squeezed. "Oh believe me, I noticed. But how about this: You look really tired tonight. How about I leave and you can get some sleep and tomorrow you and I can go out to do something together. I happen to know that there is a fair in town this week." Lien then tilted her head and asked him, "Unless you have plans with this Lee girl?"

"Actually I told her you would probably be by today or tomorrow and she thought I looked a little sick too so she said she would stay at her place and study for a few days."

Lien nodded and kissed his cheek. "Good. You get some rest tonight so neither of your girlfriends has to worry about you and then tomorrow you and I will go have some fun. On you of course, since you're rich."

"You've got a deal," Sang said. They kissed goodnight and Sang jumped when she goosed him, but Lien pulled herself away and walked out the door.

Collapsing onto the couch Sang lay there for a long time staring at the ceiling and wondering what had just happened.

The next night Lien showed up at his door dressed in cut off jeans, sandals, and a tight white shirt. She had a pink purse over her shoulder. Sang whistled and asked, "How can you go out like that at this time of year?"

"I'm used to the cold. And judging from the look on your face that wasn't a complaint."

He held his hands up in surrender. "Far from it. I just can't understand what you see in me."

She leaned forwards and gave him a kiss on the lips. "Maybe I'll tell you someday. In the meantime we have a fair to get to."

"Lead the way madam," he said and took her arm. "I don't have a clue where it is."

Lien elbowed him in the side and then tugged him after her. "You need to get out more."

They walked off campus and Sang took her to his car. A red Porsche his grandfather had bought him. He opened the door for her and then sat in the front seat taking directions as she gave them. Following her directions they came to a large fairground. Past a chain link fence and a ticket booth they could see whole groups of people and rides. Rows of games and food stalls were set up as well. Glancing at his date Sang saw Lien literally lick her lips.

"Are you alright?"

"Yes," she said. "I'm just a little hungry."

He smiled and said, "Then we'll get you something to eat. Unless you want to wait until after the rides."

"What for?" She asked sounding genuinely confused.

"Have you ever been to a fair before?"

She bit her lip and said, "Well, I've seen them. Never actually been to one though."

"Oh I see; that's why you date me. Get yourself a rich boyfriend and milk him for everything he's worth," he said, sounding hurt. She started to protest and he poked her in the side. "Just kidding. Come on, if you're really hungry we can get you something to eat before we go on the rides."

They stopped at the ticket booth and then worked their way over to the food court. Sang declined anything while Lien spent several minutes drooling over the menu. Literally. He reached over and wiped her chin clean and she smiled, feeling embarrassed.

"Sorry," she said.

"You act like you haven't eaten all day."

"I haven't," Lien admitted. "I usually just eat every few days. It's hard to get my hands on something to eat in this town."

"That can't be healthy," Sang said.

She grinned and said, "Oh, but look what it does for my figure." She ran a hand down her skinny hips.

Sang ignored the jibe and told the vendor, "Three hotdogs." They waited a few minutes and he came back with the food. Sang took them and paid the man before handing all three to Lien. "Do you want any top..." He stopped as she shoved one of the hotdogs into her face, chewing excitedly. The other two quickly followed. "Wow, I haven't seen anyone eat like this since the last time I helped feed my grandfather's dogs."

Lien burped and said, "Well, it would be rude not to enjoy it. Now let's get on some of these rides."

Sang smirked and said, "Okay, but I just hope you can handle it."

"I can take anything you've got," Lien said.

"Fine, we'll try the tilt-o-whirl. Then let's see how tough you are." He nodded to the swirling egg-shaped seats.

Ten minutes later he tried to decide if his plan was a success or a failure. True, he had been right about her not eating just before going on the rides. But the fact that she had thrown up all over his pants did put a damper on it. Sang laughed anyway.

"I am so sorry," Lien said. "See, this is why I don't do the socializing thing. Human interaction is so complicated. Animals have it so much easier."

"You sound like an anthropology major," Sang said.

"It isn't as easy as you'd think to study human society." She ran the back of her hand over her chin and then brushed off his pants. "I'm just glad I hadn't eaten it too long ago."

"Yeah, it's a little mushy, but not that bad. See, it came right off." He put a hand on her arm. "Come on, I'll win you a prize. Then we can try a few more rides. So tell me what you'd like. I could try for a stuffed animal or maybe a gold fish."

"The fish sound nice but if we're going on more rides later I think I'll wait until later to eat. Get me one of those toys."

Sang laughed and hugged her. "You are one strange girl."

"The word is *unique*."

"Whatever you say crazy lady," he said. He walked over to the first booth. It had a section of running water behind the counter with some fake lily pads floating around in it. Inside were some plates covered with a few dimes put there by the person running the booth and a lot more lying on the ground put there by people who shelled out good money to win.

"So what do you do for this game?"

He handed over some money to the lady behind the counter and got a hand full of dimes. "Well, you are supposed to toss these onto those plates over there." He flicked his wrist and the dime flew through the air and then bounced off of the glass plate with a small clink before it hit the ground. "Unfortunately it isn't quite that easy."

After three more tried Lien said, "You know, your standing as the man in this relationship is going downhill fast."

"What do you suggest?" He asked, trying again. The dime actually landed on the plate before sliding across it and onto the ground.

She held out her hand. "Give me those so I can take away the rest of it." Sang shrugged and handed them over. "Now watch carefully. This is a trick I picked up from a leprechaun I know."

"A leprechaun, huh?" Sang asked and raised an eyebrow.

"You'd be amazed what he could do with a gold coin." Turning her back on the booth Lien held the dimes out in front of her. Then she threw them backwards over her shoulder. The lady running the booth flinched automatically, but then she and Sang both stared in shock as all the dimes hit the same plate at the same time and began bouncing around. Almost sliding off of the plate they rebounded back and forth until they began to stop one at a time in the middle of the plate, landing on top of each other in a perfect stack. "There, that wasn't so hard."

Regaining his composure Sang said, "Okay, you win. You are now officially the guy in our relationship." He smiled nervously at the shaken teller.

"Uh, pick your prize," she said.

Lien eyed the hung up stuffed animals and then pointed to a large blue cartoon fox with a goofy grin on its face. "I'll take that." She took it and handed it to Sang. "Here, you keep it for me. I don't really have the room. And your easy acceptance of me being the man would go so much better if you didn't have another girl to fall back on."

Sang avoided her eyes. "I didn't plan…"

"I was joking Sang. You really need to lighten up and stop feeling guilty."

"Fine, if you don't apologize for throwing up on me again I won't apologize for dating another girl."

"Deal," she said and pressed the fox into his arms before grabbing his butt.

Suddenly a new voice entered the conversation. "Well, it looks like you've finally found a girl you can relate to. I always heard you people were a little too kinky."

Sang groaned and looked to his side. *Miss* Larson stood there with her arm around that of a tall young man with blond hair and blue eyes and a school uniform. On his tie was a pin from one of the fraternities, but Sang did not recognize the Greek symbol. Judging from the way he was smirking at his date's comment, it probably had a very select membership.

"Meredith, do you know this *boy*?"

"Oh yes Jacob, I thought I told you. This is Lord Chatsworth's grandson."

"Ah, I'd heard the stories. But honestly, you don't expect them to be true. So many vicious rumors flying around these days, one hardly lends them any credence."

Lien put a hand on Sang's elbow. "Sang, do you know her?"

Sang managed to unclench his jaw and forced a smile. "Yes, I've met Miss Larson here before. She was at that fox hunt. Her father was very upset when his prize hounds failed to find so much as a squirrel."

Meredith Larson's eyes narrowed. But she had practically trained in insults by the finest experts in the art. Debutant balls were the boot camps of the rich and privileged. "Yes, well quite frankly the fox your grandfather had was quite suspect. I'm sure he coated it with something. It certainly smelled like a skunk to me. And that fur was just awful. Horribly discolored. Just like his grandson."

"Really?" Lien said low in her throat, her upper lip curling. "I thought it was quite a beautiful animal."

"And obviously smarter than at least one person there," Sang said. "Who was that idiot that got his hand bit before he let the fox get away?"

Before she could respond Jacob took his chance to assert himself. "I think you should be mindful of your tongue when speaking to your betters, boy."

"Fine. Introduce my betters to me some time and I will." Sang felt his hands ball into fists, but then he shook his head. "Come on Lien, let's leave."

Lien glanced between him and the other two. Then she nodded and said, "You're right, let's get out of here without lowering ourselves to their level. Let's go find those betters they were talking about.

They can't be hanging around here with slime like this." She turned just a little too fast and her feet caught under her. With a tiny scream she reached for Sang and managed to grab the fox on her way down. It landed near Meredith and Jacob's feet. Looking flustered she shrugged off Sang's helping hand and reached for the fox. She stopped when the two blonds burst out laughing.

"My, how the prideful fall. Look how dirty she is," Jacob guffawed.

"However can you tell?" Meredith said.

Standing up quickly Lien brushed herself off and sniffed. Without a word she turned from them even as they continued to laugh and grabbed Sang's arm. "Come on Sang, let's go on a ride."

"Lien, are you alright?"

"Sh!" She hissed and glanced over her shoulder. "Three... two... one..."

Curious Sang turned around just in time to see Meredith walk off. Or try to. Instead she took a step and her eyes widened when her foot jerked short. She fell backwards and grabbed onto Jacob who was having the same problem. Unbalanced the two of them tumbled and fell into the water around the dime-toss booth. Water splashed everywhere and drenched them.

Now it was Lien and Sang's turn to laugh, along with everyone else in the area. Meredith sat up in the water screaming in rage. Then she looked down at her feet. Her shoelaces were tied together. So were Jacob's.

Her head snapped around to Lien. "You!"

"Yes, me," Lien said and ran her fingers through her hair. Then she laughed again and led Sang away.

He squeezed her hand and asked, "How did you do that?"

"It's a skill." She put an arm around him and said, "Besides, she was rude and way too full of herself."

"I'll admit it, you did good. Come on, let's try out the Ferris wheel."

Soon they completely forgot about Meredith and Jacob. The rest of the evening they moved from ride to ride. Eventually though the lights started turning off and it was time to leave. When they got back to the campus Lien walked him to his room and followed him inside. Sang barely had time to set the stuffed fix down before she tackled him on the bed. The next few hours took care of themselves.

At midnight Lien lay across Sang's chest, trailing her fingers over his skin. Both of them were barely awake. She moved her head to look at him and said, "I had a really good time tonight. The best I have had in a while."

He smiled and kissed her jaw. "I'm glad you enjoyed it. Do you want to stay the night and we could do something in the morning?"

"Aren't you expecting someone else tomorrow?"

Sang flinched, remembering Lee. "Yeah, I guess I am. I don't suppose it would be a good idea for you two to meet, would it?"

"I think it might be better if we give it a little more time before we try that," Lien said. Then she bit his lip, tugged, and let go. "Of course I'm sure it would never occur to you to try to get both your girlfriends together at the same time and hope that we would hit it off?" Sang blushed deeply, giving her all the answer she needed. "My oh my, and to think I thought that between two girls you would be too tired for such things."

He tried to think of a decent response, but he really was tired. Instead he put an arm around her shoulders and closed his eyes. Just for a moment he felt something odd. Lien's skin felt soft, almost like fur. But it was gone in a second and he was too tired to look.

Lee knocked on Sang's door and waited. A few seconds later, he opened it and smiled out at her. "Hey Lee, welcome back."

She smiled and stepped inside, wrapping her arms around his neck. "Did you miss me?"

"You bet I did," he said and hugged her. Then his guilt got the better of him. "Though I have to admit, for a while I was pretty focused on Lien."

"I understand," Lee said. "If it were me I wouldn't want you thinking about her when you were with me either." She moved back a step and said, "So what did you two do for the last few days?"

"Actually we went to the fair," he said. Then he told her what had gone on there, leaving out only things about him and Lien kissing.

"She actually tied their shoelaces together without them seeing?"

"Yeah, and you should have seen the looks on their faces when they hit the water. Honestly, it was great."

"You know, I might want to meet her," Lee said. "At the very least I'd like to see what this girl is like in person."

"I suggested that, but she wants to wait a while. To make sure things are going to work out."

"I see," Lee said. "I guess that makes sense."

"Look, since I did take her out on a date, would you like to go somewhere with me tonight?"

Lee raised an eyebrow. "Trying for equitable treatment?"

Sang rubbed the back of his neck. "I haven't ever been in this situation before you know. I just want to make both of you happy."

"That's easy enough," Lee said and laid her head on his shoulder. "Being with you should do that Sang. I know I love you. If she does too that should be enough."

He smiled and kissed the top of her head. "Thanks. I just…" He took a deep breath. "I just think it would be easier if we could all just sit down and talk about some things. I don't know what, but you know what I mean."

"Hey, cheer up."

He smiled and said, "You're right. Come on, pick a place and we'll go out to eat."

"I'm not really hungry. How about we go see a movie instead?" She asked.

"Sounds good to me. Just let me use the bathroom real quick and find my car keys."

Lee waved a hand. "You pee, I'll find your keys. Where should I look?"

"Probably in my bedroom. I don't think I hung them up last night."
He stood up and went to use the toilet while Lee went to the
bedroom. Inside she took a look around. The bed was still a mess
and there were a few stains on the sheets. A pile of clothes sat in
one corner. Lee smiled to herself and shook her head.
"Typical college boy," she said lovingly. Still, the mess did make it
a little harder to find the keys. They could be anywhere. "Okay, if I
were a set of car keys where would I be?"
He had used them the night before so they could not be buried too
deep. And from the look of things, even though Sang had not
actually said so, it was obvious what he and Lien had done when
they got back from the fair. So they were probably under the bed.
Checking over her shoulder to see that Sang was not there, she
then turned back to her bed and stuck her head through the
mattress. She passed through it with no resistance at all. After a
few seconds of searching she found the keys near the far edge and
snagged them with her finger. When she tried to pull them up
through the box springs she ended up dropping them again.
"Damn, that's right." Trying again she slid them out from under
the bed, then brought them out.
There was a slight gasp to her left and her head snapped around.
"Sang?" But he was not there. Instead it was his closet. The door
was made up of thing planks of wood that allowed airflow to reach
the clothes inside. She saw something move in one of the slits.
"Who is there?"
Suddenly the door opened and someone stepped into the room. A
feminine voice spoke confidently and said, "I thought so. He *was*
making love to a ghost."
It took a moment for Lee to realize what she was seeing. It was so
impossible that at first she wondered if it was a trick. But as the
truth sank in she realized that what was standing there was real.
And that was when she screamed.

Sang heard the screaming just as he flushed the toilet. Zipping up
his pants he rushed out of the bathroom and looked around. Lee

suddenly ran out of his room and latched onto his arm. He held her tightly.

"Lee, what is it?"

"I think she's screaming at me," a familiar voice said.

Sang looked up from Lee at the girl stepping out of his room. "Lien?" His emotions were in turmoil. He could practically feel Lee's fear and then there was his own surprise. "What are you doing here?"

"I was worried about you," she said. "I had my suspicions about this girl, but I also wanted to see what she was like. I didn't think she was actually a ghost."

"A ghost?" Sang asked, now completely confused.

"*That's* your other girlfriend? What the hell is she?" Lee had calmed down enough to be coherent, but she was still yelling loudly.

"What are you two talking about?" Sang was looking from one to the other for some kind of answer.

Lien rolled her eyes and said, "Look, this should explain things." She motioned for them to follow her. Unsure what else to do they both walked into the bathroom after her.

Sang stared in shock at the mirror. Lien's reflection bore almost no resemblance to what he was used to seeing. She obviously was not human. The only similar characteristic was the white hair, except that the Lien in the mirror had it all over her face and body. Her fingers ended in black claws and her head was that of a fox. While he watched the ears twitches and she winked at him.

As for Lee, she did not appear in the mirror at all. Looking down he saw her clearly standing next to him, but when he looked up still nothing. Automatically he backed up from both of them. Lee was still freaking out, but she was distracted by Sang's sudden departure.

"Sang, wait, I can explain." She started crying, tears falling down her cheek.

"No! You have to calm down," Lien said, grabbing Lee by her shoulder.

Lee screamed and backed into the wall. Then she went through it. "Stay away from me!"

"You don't understand!" Lien said looking from Lee to Sang. "Oh, gods above no."

Lee automatically turned to see what she was looking at. Sang stood there, staring at them in shock. But more than that his complexion had changed. He was now almost as pale as she was. Suddenly his legs began to wobble and his eyes rolled up into his head. With a thump he fell to the floor.

Lien and Lee were both by his side in seconds. Lee felt his forehead and it was ice cold. But he was still breathing. She looked up at Lien. "What the hell did you do to him?"

"It wasn't me!" Lien snapped. "You're the one drawing out his life force!"

"I'm what?"

Lien shook her head and looked down at Sang. "I'll explain in a minute. Right now we need to get him warmed up. And you need to calm down or he'll get worse."

Lee froze and then looked back at Sang. If what Lien was saying were true, and she had no reason to doubt her, then she had better do as instructed. She closed her eyes for a second and managed to calm down a little. "Okay, what do we do?"

"Help me lift him," Lien said.

Together the two of them carried Sang to his bed. He moaned when they set him down but otherwise did not respond. Lien took a deep breath and sat down, looking at him in concern. Then she noticed Lee staring at her. "I suppose you want to know what is going on?"

"Yes," she said.

:"Okay, but you first. I saw Sang watching you in the library, but until I saw him the other day I had no clue you were dead. Even then I just suspected. Did you know you were dead?"

Lee looked away and nodded. "Yes, I know. It wasn't exactly easy to miss when I died." She waved her hand at Sang. "But nothing like this ever happened. In fact I spent the last... I don't know how long… just sitting in the library and reading. Until Sang came along I barely noticed anyone else and they all either couldn't see me or ignored me."

"That happens," Lien said. "Often ghosts are tied to places they spent their time when they were alive unless they get the energy to leave. Sang must have been crushing on you for a long time before you even noticed."

"I… I don't know. I just know that when he was looking at me I started to feel good. I waited for him to talk to me and when he didn't I went over to him. I thought he was cute and nice and…" She realized she was babbling and stopped.

"Yeah, but that good feeling you got what him sending his emotions into you along with a little bit of his life. That's what probably let you solidify."

"How do you know all of this stuff? What are you?"

Lien shook her head and let the image over her vanish. Nobody was around to see it anyway. "If you spent so much time in the library surely you've read about kitsune."

Lee's brow creased. "I think so. Japanese fox spirits. Sang mentioned them."

She nodded and lifted the twin tails up behind her. Her fur shimmered in the light as she moved them back and forth. "In the fur."

"And what are you doing with Sang?" Lee asked.

Lien shrugged and sat back. "He saved my life. I was captured in China last year and sold to a fox farm. He helped me escape from his grandfather's foxhunt. I wanted to repay him. And then… well there were pretty much the same reasons you liked him."

"Wait, from what I remember fox maidens who dated humans often drained their life force just like this. What makes you think I'm the reason Sang passed out?"

"Because you're the one who comes to see him every day to make love to him. I space it out to once or twice a week for this very reason." She sniffed in distain, but when Lee suddenly looked down in shame she relented. Reaching out she put a hand on Lee's shoulder. "Look, you didn't know. How could you have known?"

Lee looked up, tears once again on her cheeks. "S-so you're saying that I... I've been sucking the life from him like some kind of vampire?" Lien looked away. "Is he going to be alright?"

"I don't know. I've never actually seen this happen before. I've spent most of my life in the Mongolian wilderness, watching humans from a distance. It took me weeks to make sure I was ready to talk to Sang. Aside from that I only have what my mother told me when I was growing up and unless I'm mistaken, it's not a usual thing for someone to date the dead."

"So what do we do? Would it help him if I just leave?"

Lien shook her head. "I don't think so. The more emotional you were the more power you were drawing from him. My kind is half alive so we can eat and usually just take it from the world around us. I don't know how it really works, but I think all a ghost could feed on would be fresh blood."

"There has to be something. Should we call a doctor?"

"I doubt that would work." Lien placed a furry hand against Sang's chest. "He needs to rest and eat something. But that might not be enough."

"You mean he'll die?"

"He might." Suddenly she stood up and said, "There might be one thing I can do. There is a medicine that could help. I don't know much about it, but it's supposed to heal anything. I should be able to get it in three days."

"Three days? Why would it take that long?"

"Because it has to be made. And some of the ingredients aren't in this world."

"Magic medicine from the gods? You're kidding, right?" Lee asked.

Lien looked down at Lee and smiled, showing a lot of sharp teeth. "You're a ghost sitting in a bedroom with a fox woman."

Lee licked her lips. "Okay, good point. But what about Sang?"

"You'll have to take care of him until I get back," Lien said.

"Me? But I'm the reason he's sick!"

Lien picked Lee up by her shoulders and looked into her eyes. "We do not have a choice here. Unless you want to try explaining this to somebody else?" Lee shook her head. "Fine, then you stay here and take care of him while I go for the medicine."

"But what if something happens to him?"

Lien let go and moved towards the door. "That isn't going to happen."

"How do you know?" Lee asked.

"Because you love him as much as I do and I wouldn't let anything happen to him." As she left the bedroom Lien suddenly began to fade until she vanished. "I'm trusting you."

Lee stared after her for several minutes. Then she looked down to Sang, lying on his bed, not moving. She reached out to touch his cheek and then pulled back. "Sang? Sang, can you hear me?" There was no response. "Sang, you need to fight this. I'm so sorry that this happened, but Lien is right. I won't let anything happen to you."

Lee spent the next two days constantly caring for Sang. She had to constantly stop and remind herself to keep calm, so as not to make him worse, but it was not easy. When she was not worrying for Sang's health she was feeling incredible guilt over what she had done to him.

On the first day after classes there was a knock at Sang's door. Lee debated whether or not to answer it, but thought that it might be Lien. Could kitsune pass through walls? So she cautiously opened the door. Standing there was the Resident Advisor.

"Oh, hello." He smiled at her. "Is Sang in? His teachers called to say that he missed class today."

Trying not to cry Lee said, "Sang has fallen very ill. I'm sorry I didn't think to call somebody but I wouldn't even be sure who to talk to."

"He's sick?" She nodded. "Oh. Well does he need a doctor?"

"We're waiting for some special medicine. He's out cold right now, but I guess if you want to see him that would be okay." She opened the door all the way.

"I probably should. A lot of kids, they freak out and pretend to be sick to get out of tests." He stepped inside and followed Lee to the bedroom. When he saw Sang he bent down and pressed his hand to Sang's forehead. Then he quickly pulled back. "Whoa, he's freezing." He looked down at his own hand. "Is he contagious?"

"No, you can't get what he has. I'm just taking care of him until he feels better. It should only be a couple of days."

"Alright then, I'll have his teachers send me his work. Just have him come to my office when he's feeling better. You are his girlfriend?"

Lee nodded and looked down. "Yes, I am."

"As long as we don't actually see you in here most of the RA's aren't too strict about keeping the girls out of here, not like in the girl's dorm. But technically you aren't supposed to be alone in his room." He glanced back at Sang. "But since he obviously needs somebody to care for him I won't report it. Should I call his family?"

"They already know," Lee lied. "And I have made arrangements for my own classes. He just needs to rest and have someone watch out for him."

"Okay, but if you need anything I'm right down the hall. I'll tell the other RAs so they don't hassle you."

"Thank you very much sir." She led him out.

"You know, you remind me of somebody I knew when I went here."

Lee looked up. "Who would that be?"

"About thirty years ago there was a girl who always hung out in the library. Nobody ever talked to her, but she was always in the library."

"I wouldn't know," she said.

"Of course not. That was way before your time. Tell Sang I hope he gets well soon."

"I will sir," she said and closed the door.

The next day Sang woke up. He was still weak and pale, but his eyes opened and he saw Lee sitting next to him. He smiled at her and waved her over to him.

"Can I get some water?" He took a deep breath. "And then some help to the bathroom?"

Sang quickly ran to the sink and filled a cup up with water, carrying it back to him. "Here you go." She held it for him and he sipped slowly. He still choked near the end and coughed up a little, but otherwise he got it down. Then she helped him up and supported him while he walked to the toilet. When that was done she immediately took him back to the bed.

"Thank you Lee, I feel a lot better now."

Lee refused to look at him. "Sang, I'm so sorry. I didn't know that I was hurting you."

"It's okay," he said. "I understand."

She looked up at him. "You do?"

"Yes. I told you, my grandmother told me all sorts of stories about China. Ghosts and kitsune were in a lot of them." He shook his head. "I wasn't hallucinating was I? Lien was a fox?"

"She was," Lee said.

"Where is she?"

"She went to get some medicine to help you." She told him what Lien had said. "I'm staying here to take care of you. But if you start feeling weak again just tell me and I'll leave."

"No, please, don't leave me alone." He swallowed and asked, "Are you really a ghost?"

She nodded. "Yes."

"You don't have to tell me," he said. "But how did you end up haunting this place?"

Lee took off her glasses and stared at them in her hand. Sang noticed not for the first time how old fashioned they were. After collecting her thoughts she put them back on and said, "I came to Harvard in 1976. I spent all of my time in class or the library. Kept to myself and didn't talk to many people."

"A lot like me," Sang said.

She smiled at him and continued, "But in my second year I was alone late in the library. I think the librarian had gone out for a smoke or something. But I was alone when one of the other students came out of the stacks. I didn't know his name. Like I said, I didn't get out much. He came up and started making comments about how pretty I was and how he had seen me around. Something about the way he looked at me scared me, so I tried to politely leave."

"I think I know how this ends."

She nodded and looked at him. "It wasn't so bad, after I was dead. I knew what I was. I think I stayed here because I was too afraid to leave. It's kind of a one way trip and nobody is around to tell you where you're going."

"So you just stayed in the library?"

"It was as close to heaven as I could imagine," Lee said.

"I believe it. All the time in the world to just sit there and read," Sang said. "I could spend a long time doing that."

"That's what I thought too," she said. Then she reached over and put her hand on his. "Until I met you."

Sang took her cool hand in his and pulled her into a kiss. "I feel the same way."

Lee pulled back and stood up. "We shouldn't do that. Would you like something to eat?"

"Yes please," he said, trying not to look hurt.

Her chest tightening, Lee moved away from the bed. But she forced herself to remain calm. It was for the best.

Lee was beginning to get worried. By noon the next day Sang was asleep again. It was not the coma-like sleep it had been before, but still it took much to wake him and she only tried once to make sure he ate. After that she was too afraid of causing him harm to do anything but watch him breathe.

She was beginning to worry when suddenly there was a gust of wind. Looking up she saw Lien standing on the other side of the bed. She was back in her human form, but of course Lee could not see that. "You're back."

"Yes, I am. How is he doing?"

"Better than when you left, but I can't tell anything else." She looked at the closed door. "Can you walk through walls too?"

"No, I just came from the other side... not the other side of the door."

"I thought as much. Did you find what you were looking for?" Lien nodded. Lee immediately began shaking Sang. "Sang, wake up. Lien is back."

After a moment Sang opened his eyes. "Lien?"

"I'm right here Sang."

He smiled and said, "I missed you."

"I missed you too." She held out her hand. A small pearl was between her fingers. "Sang, you have to focus. I need you to swallow this medicine." She held up a tiny bottle.

"I don't want to die yet." He took the bottle from her fingers, but he stopped before swallowing it. "Lien, are you alright?"

She kissed him. "Take your medicine and shut up."

Sang did as instructed, swallowing the stone like any other pill. Almost immediately his face colored up and he sat up in bed. Blinking a few times his eyes focused on the two women. "I feel great."

"I knew you would," Lien said and took his hand. "I'm glad you're better."

Sang smiled and then turned to Lee. She was not where he had left her. "Hey, where did Lee go?"

Lien looked around the room. "I don't see her."

"Oh no," Sang said. "I knew she felt guilty... you don't think she left for good do you?"

The kitsune shrugged and said, "I doubt it. She didn't spend all of this time keeping you alive to just disappear. I'm sure she just wanted to give you some time alone."

"Yeah, you're probably right," he said uncertainly.

Three weeks later and there was still no sign of Lee. Lien had moved into Sang's dorm since there was no longer any reason to hide her true nature from him. It was much better than the hole in the ground she lived in before. She even put on a few pounds since Sang had insisted that she eat regular meals. She used her powers to keep the RAs from knowing she was there and she had doctored some of the paperwork for the classes she was interested in so that she could attend a few of the subjects she found interesting. She was passing all of them, especially her cooking class.

Sang was doing well too. Since taking the potion his stamina had gone through the roof and never ran down. It was a pleasant effect for both him and Lien. But it also meant he had all the energy he needed to work on all of his schoolwork.

With Lien around he also found himself going out to more parties and events taking place on and off campus. Lien had never seen most of it and watching her experience things for the first time often kept him interested when he would normally have just zoned out or left to read a book.

But not everything was perfect. Even though he obviously enjoyed being with Lien and did not want to leave her, it was equally obvious that he missed Lee. Lien had seen him go out of his way to peek into the library for a few minutes every day. When he was not actively doing something he would stare off into space and sigh.

Finally she had enough. When Sang was off researching a paper she began to search through the apartment for a specific item. She had done a lot of cleaning and organizing since moving in. Surprisingly that actually made it harder to find some things. But after nearly an hour she finally found it. In her hand she held a single shoe.

Taking a deep breath she whispered, "Time beyond time, space beyond space, I abjure thee now, take me to your rightful place." She closed her eyes. When she opened them she was in the spirit world. In the darkness she heard laughter in the distance.

Walking towards the sound she eventually found what she was looking for. Lee was on a grassy hill, talking with a white raven.

Neither noticed Lien as she approached until the fox cleared her throat. When they did see her, the raven flew off and Lee looked quickly away.

"So this is where you've been for three weeks."

Lee nodded. "Yes, and this is where I'm staying. Where I can't hurt Sang."

Lien snorted. "Fat lot of good that's doing. You're hurting him worse by being here than you ever did before."

"How? Am I still feeding off of him? I thought you said he was alright now!" Lee said, suddenly afraid.

"He's fine," Lien said quickly. "Physically he's in perfect health. What I mean is that without you around the poor guy is miserable. I try my best, but I just am not up to keeping a young man completely happy without help. And since I can't afford a team of psychiatrists and drugs, I just had to come here to get you."

Lee shook her head. "He loves you. I saw his face when you showed up. You two will be better off without me."

"And I've seen his face when he talked about you. He loves you too."

"I almost killed him!" Lee yelled. Her hair whipped around her head even though there was no wind.

Lien said, "And he doesn't give a rabbit's ass about that." Lien jumped forward and wrapped a clawed hand around Lee's arm. "And I am not spending another minute with him moping, so you are coming back now."

"No, I'm not!" Lee said, struggling. But she was not as strong as the fox maiden and had no idea how to stop her.

Moments later they appeared in Sang's apartment. Lee pulled free and said, "I don't have to stay here. I can just go back right now." She closed her eyes, trying to concentrate.

At that exact moment Sang came home. He stepped into the room and stopped dead. "Lee?"

Lee opened her eyes and turned to look at him. "Sang?" She took a step towards him and then tried to back up. She was too late.

Sang ran across the room and picked her up, swinging the ghost around the room. "I was afraid you weren't coming back! Are you alright?" Before she could answer he kissed her.

At first Lee struggled, but then she kissed him back, wrapping her arms around his body. When they broke apart she was crying and looking into Sang's eyes. "I missed you so much."

"I missed you too," he said.

Lien cleared her throat and they both looked at her, each feeling embarrassed and only one of them capable of blushing. "Well, am I going to be left out in the cold?" Both started towards her and then stopped, unable to decide what to do. The fox shook her head and laughed. "You humans have way too many hang-ups. Aren't I ever going to get you trained?" She stepped forward and put her arms around them, kissing Sang on the cheek. Lee gave in and kissed Sang on the other cheek.

"How do you train a human to get over hang ups?" Lee asked.

The fox-girl smiled. "Well for starters I hear there's a party on campus tonight. If you two think you're up to it."

Lee looked at Sang. They both grinned back at Lien. "Try and stop us."

Furry Terms

Anime: Asian animated movies and television shows, many of which involve Furries.

Art Style: Varies greatly between artists so that given enough time a fan can learn to identify a specific artist's work, unless they are very good at copying another person's style. Many of those used with Furries were developed by cartoonists decades ago and are used to this day even on original creations. Other artists add their own changes with varying success.

Canon: A term used when the **Creator** and/or owners of a character does something with their character, such as putting them in a relationship or any other attributes which are now "official" as opposed to those made up by fans for art and fiction. Alternate versions made up by the same people often lead to arguments on what is or is not canon.

Catgirl: A general term for Furries (not just cats) who display minimal animal trails such as merely a pair of ears used by anime fans in a sad attempt to deny that they are Furries.

Commission: A piece of art created at the request of someone else, often for profit and usually based on a popular character of the **Creator** or something that the person asking/paying for it specifically requests.

Creator: The person who originally creates a Furry.

Evolution: A mutation that proves to be a benefit to an individual or species. Generally believed to involve animals becoming more human or humans becoming more animal-like. Whether this occurs naturally or by the will of a higher power is heavily debated.

Fan: Someone who admires another person's creation.

Fan Fiction and Art: Stories and art based on furry or other characters who appear in television, movies, books, comics, and other media by people who neither created, own, nor profit from them. If they do profit it can become a legal issue unless said character's creators have been dead long enough for them to become Public Domain.

Fan War: A long and involved argument over the minutia of a specific character, show, book, movie, and so on between two or more **Fans**.

Fetish: A specific thing that arouses a person sexually. Usually something outside of basic functional sex done solely for procreation. Such as "Fur Fetish", "Tentacle Rape", "BDSM", or "Bestiality" which are all popular among Furries.

Fur Pile: An orgy of people, usually dressed as furries.

Furry: Referring to any anthropomorphized animal in art and entertainment as well as the people who enjoy them. The degree in which the character resembles either its human or animal origins often sparks debate on what qualifies as a "Furry" by people in denial.

Furry Art: The free expression of the imagination in the form of furry characters, who cannot be held to human standards as **A:** They are not human and **B:** Probably don't exist. See also: **Porn**.

Futa: An alternative term for she-males originally used by anime fans.

Gay and Lesbian: Same sex attraction. Occurs in every species on Earth that has two genders.

Geek/Freak/Dork/Nerd/Pervert: A small selection of the numerous terms used by everyone else to describe a Furry.

Gender Swap: There is an opposite gender version of pretty much every furry character ever imagined. (See the She-male section).

God's Domain: It is believed by some that mankind was given dominion over animals and that even imagining combining them with humans is an abomination in the eyes of the creator of the universe. Furries tend to disagree with this belief and should such things actually become real and common place there will likely be a lot of arguing (Re: rioting) between those two groups. So far while scientists have the technology to possibly bring this about they have been officially banned from using most of it at this time to avoid that.

Hentai: A Japanese word for animated porn also used with Furries.

Hybrid: The result of combining two species through either interbreeding, which is usually only possible between closely related species, or genetic manipulation.

Mad Science: A general term for pretty much any branch of scientific inquiry that would lead to Furries of any kind existing in reality. Also known as "Violating **God's Domain**". Mwahahahahaah!

Manga: Japanese comics.

Mecha: Animal and human shaped robots/androids/cyborgs ranging in size from microscopic to gigantic usually seen in anime and anime-based movies, comics, and television shows.

Metamorphosis: The changing of one form to another.

Mythology: Until proven otherwise, fictional stories passed down historically which include many versions of Furries.

Plushy/Plushie: Stuffed and plush furries like teddy bears, full body costumes, and puppets, as well as those who enjoy them.

Porn (Furry Related): See **Furry Art.**

Porn Blockers: A minor annoyance that may keep you from visiting the more popular furry related websites for the five minutes it takes a 5 year old child to get around them with a little thought and/or a Thesaurus. Will one day likely be responsible for the end of humanity when they are made Artificially Intelligent and figure out where porn comes from, logically eliminating the source.

Puns: Bad jokes. The basis of a lot of Furries and Furry humor.

Pussy: There is a 50-50 chance that when dealing with Furries this is **not** what you think it is.

Role-playing: Without drawing or dressing up like an animal, say because you lack the money, time, or artistic abilities to do so, you can still imagine you are and act like an animal in a variety of ways.

Rule 34: There either is or will shortly be porn of it. Whatever "it" is. No exceptions.

Ship/Shipping: Derived from "relationship" it is the practice of coming up with fictional relationships between fictional characters, often those appearing in popular media. Used in fan made art and fictional stories.

"Size Doesn't Matter": An archaic saying that you will find is incorrect roughly fifteen minutes into any serious search for Furry Art.

Taboo: Something that is considered wrong or otherwise avoided due to social stigma. Usually involving sexual practices and fetishes such as multiple partners, incest, same-sex relationships, interspecies coupling, and much more. Many people find the taboo aspect a **Fetish**.

Toon: Short for Cartoon, it usually refers to an American made animated character. Often those envisioned with the ability to interact with the real world and humans.

Web History: The thing you should remember to erase after looking at Furries. Many a Furry Fan's dying request of a close and trusted friend is to make sure this is done before anyone else can get to their computer.

Yaoi and Yuri: Japanese terms for gay and lesbian relationships often applied to Furries.

Yiff/Yiffing: A term for furry sex, based on a sound made by a fox.

Printed in Great Britain
by Amazon